T0198646

FLYING WITH
One Wing

God's Grace in Our Times of Adversity

Pamula Yerby-Hammack

authorHOUSE®

AuthorHouse™
1663 Liberty Drive
Bloomington, IN 47403
www.authorhouse.com
Phone: 1 (800) 839-8640

Published by AuthorHouse 01/24/2018

ISBN: 978-1-5462-2571-3 (sc)
ISBN: 978-1-5462-2572-0 (e)

Print information available on the last page.

This book is printed on acid-free paper.

King James Version (KJV)
Public Domain

New International Version (NIV)
*Holy Bible, New International Version®, NIV® Copyright ©1973, 1978, 1984,
2011 by Biblica, Inc.® Used by permission. All rights reserved worldwide.*

New Living Translation (NLT)
*Holy Bible, New Living Translation, copyright © 1996, 2004, 2007, 2013,
2015 by Tyndale House Foundation. Used by permission of Tyndale House
Publishers Inc., Carol Stream, Illinois 60188. All rights reserved.*

New American Standard Bible (NASB)
*Copyright © 1960, 1962, 1963, 1968, 1971, 1972, 1973,
1975, 1977, 1995 by The Lockman Foundation*

English Standard Version (ESV)
*The Holy Bible, English Standard Version. ESV® Text Edition: 2016. Copyright ©
2001 by Crossway Bibles, a publishing ministry of Good News Publishers.*

CONTENTS

DEDICATION

I would like to dedicate this book to my Lord and Savior Jesus, the Christ, for His unselfish death on the cross and His triumphant resurrection from the grave for me. He is the only reason I live, and I am forever committed to Him. I bow in worship and adoration before You my Lord. I love You forever.

To Mommy and Daddy, God gave me the best parents ever. Thank you for teaching me about Jesus and always exemplifying a godly life before me. Your love, prayers, and support are phenomenal and are the bedrock of my life. I am so proud and honored to be your daughter. I love you beyond words.

To Cianni, my loving and strong daughter, there are no words to express the love I have for you. When my pain became your pain and my suffering became your suffering, you showed unconditional love. No one could have done what you did. You have walked right beside me through my darkest valleys and never gave up that "Mommy will be alright." I would have to write an entire book to let you know how much you mean to me. You are one of God's best gifts to me (after Jesus of course. Wink Wink).

To my son-in-love T.C., who treated me as a precious jewel during my illness, I love you dearly.

What can I say about my grandchildren She'-Tiel, Christian, and D'Andre? You guys bring me so much joy!

I have been blessed to be part of a great sibling group. My siblings—Cindy, Cakey, Bodie, Lisa, and Richie—are my very best friends forever. Thank you for always loving me and supporting me. Do not think that I will ever stop needing you. I can't tell you how much you mean to me;

maybe these tears welling up in my eyes as I write these words will give you a hint. (Smile).

God has blessed me with more cheerleaders in my life than I can count. This book is dedicated to you too. Thank you all for your love and support:

> Wind of Change Ministries, Inc.
> City of Abraham Church and Ministries, Inc.
> Former co-workers of Kennedy Krieger Institute, especially Dr. Martha Bridge Denckla, MD.
> My special sisters Gwennie, Felicia, Dana, Gail, Pat, Paula, Kim, and Sandy (who went home to be with the Lord before this book was finished. I miss you so much Sis. See you when I get to heaven).
> Dr. V and my insightful, respectful, competent, and empathetic therapist Sharon.
> Pastors and churches throughout the Baltimore community and surrounding areas.
> All those who prayed me through.
> All those who struggle with mental health illnesses. (God will help you enjoy life in spite of it. Trust Him).

Special Thanks to:

The psychiatrists, therapists, social workers, nurses, and staff of the Sheppard Pratt Mental Hospital; Towson, MD.

In Loving Memory

I saw him from a distance in 1986, and had no clue that he would fill my life with so much joy. His love, strength, wisdom, and his presence were mine to enjoy until 2014, when God called him home to be with Him. Van Hammack, my loving husband, I still love you more than love and always will. I did not get a chance to say goodbye, but I will get to tell you hello when God calls me home. Rest well my darling. You fought a good fight, you kept the faith, and you finished your course.

"But He said to me, 'My grace is sufficient for you, for My power is made perfect in weakness.' Therefore, I will boast all the more gladly about my weaknesses, so that Christ's power may rest on me. That is why, for Christ's sake, I delight in weaknesses, in insults, in hardships, in persecutions, in difficulties. For when I am weak, then I am strong."

The Apostle Paul
2 Corinthians 12:9-10 NIV

FOREWORD

Fearless. Completely fearless. About 5 foot nothing, maybe 90 pounds wet, with a megawatt smile that could light up the East Coast. This powerhouse of energy had a laugh that was so infectious that the whole office would follow her lead. There was no getting away from the fact that in 1995, I had met someone truly phenomenal. That is what hit me when I first met Reverend Pamula Yerby-Hammack over 20 years ago. And over the year I lived in Baltimore, we became like sisters, and our sisterhood still remains.

We came from such different backgrounds. I grew up as a white woman in the 1960s in Lubbock, TX, where racial tensions did not make national news, but were certainly no less real. By contrast, Pam grew up in Baltimore where her amazing father, the dynamic pastor of St. Abraham Baptist Church on North Avenue, was himself the great grandchild of slaves. In 1995, I left everyone and everything I knew in Texas and traveled across country for a chance to train at the Johns Hopkins University for a year. Pam was literally the second person I met coming to Baltimore, the first being my employer. Pam and I connected immediately and joyfully. I did not have a church home, so she invited me to hers, St. Abraham Baptist Church. Her family adopted me as truly one of their own, for which I was so humbled and grateful.

But it was her fearlessness and her commitment to Christ and His truth, no matter the cost, that so impressed me then and through the decades we have known each other. She has so many, many gifts—singing, teaching, writing, and preaching. She has a phenomenal singing voice and has performed at the famous Apollo Theater in New York, NY, as well as many other large arenas along the east coast. One of the most memorable Martin Luther King, Jr. Day's in my life was getting to hear Pam sing

"Amazing Grace" at a local function in his honor. No other MLK Day in my memory comes close to what I experienced as I reflect upon the sheer power she brought to that room. Pam was amazing!

Even in 2015, when riots rocked Baltimore, you can probably guess, Pam was literally in the thick of it. She was on the streets ministering to the youth and promoting peace and dialogue. Her ministry didn't stop there. When I was blessed with the man God sent to me to marry, it was "Pastor Pam" who flew down to Dallas to assist in performing the ceremony.

Pamula Yerby-Hammack was an incredible person before her fight with depression. However, what she has demonstrated afterwards has taken incredible courage and faith.

In 2012, Pam knew intuitively something was very wrong. She didn't understand it, or even recognize it for a long, long, time, until depression nearly consumed her. She encountered as severe and as debilitating a depression I have seen anyone go through in my life personally or professionally. What she has done though is demonstrate what the power of faith and love from family, friends, mental health care professionals, and yes, from God our Father and His Son, Jesus, can do. This is the story she tells in her debut book *Flying with One Wing*, a powerful, intensely personal, account of her struggles with sudden onset and severe depression. She speaks candidly about her personality change, her loss of memory for small and big things, the loss of her ability to work and go to school, her often overwhelming sense of hopelessness, and then how she emerged on the other side a stronger woman and more passionate witness for Christ. This is an incredible story.

I urge you to please read this powerful and compelling story of one powerful dynamo of an African American woman's journey, through not just the struggles of deep, dark, mental isolation (what Winston Churchill would call the Black Dog of depression), but how with even greater courage, she has revealed her deeply intimate and terrifying struggles in ways only she can tell.

The mental health issues in the African American community have long been not well understood and certainly not in the context of a first-person narrative that Pam tells it as the master story teller she is. With her incredible faith that has in fact moved mountains, she shares her story and that makes this an incredible book for all people.

I am honored I can call this incredible woman my friend and my deeply loved sister in Christ.

Patricia Evans, MD, PhD, FAAN, FAAP
Dallas, TX
March 4, 2016

PREFACE

"I didn't die. I lived!
And now I'm telling the world what God did"
Psalm 118:17(MSG)

Friday, October 19, 2012, is etched in my mind as the day my life was suddenly changed forever. It was the day I found myself spiraling into a world of darkness, fear, confusion, and panic. It was a day when reason fled to the far unreachable recesses of my mind and the dark thoughts of my past fears and sadness lunged from the shadows and became my daily reality.

Seconds turned into minutes, minutes into hours, hours into days, and days into months, and still I could not understand what had happened to me and could find no relief. I know there is a song that says, "No man is an island, no man stands alone," but I could not help but feel I was on an island all by myself. Each day was filled with the fear that those horrifying moments of Friday, October 19, would repeat itself and in some ways, I guess they did as I replayed the events over and over and over again in my mind. Fear, dread, and sadness haunted me morning, noon, and night. Daytime was terrifying. Nighttime was dreadful. Anytime was frightening.

Many people in my space probably had not even noticed that something was wrong with me, and those who did notice did not really know how to help me. But there were a few who I dared to confide in. They had experienced firsthand what I was going through, and they tried to tell me I would be alright. However, their words and actions were somewhat incomprehensible to me because my daughter had become the only one my mind would allow me to trust. Finally, God sent relief!

When things just got increasingly worse, I found myself willingly walking into the crisis center of the Sheppard Pratt Mental Hospital. How had I gotten there? Was I crazy? No. I just needed some help and it was there where God had a place of healing and restoration for me. After talking to the intake psychiatrist, she concluded I was suffering from depression and anxiety and agreed I was a perfect candidate for the Sheppard Pratt Adult Day Hospital program. I was in a place I had never been before. But wanting help so much, I was willing to try anything.

On November 27, 2012, I was admitted. Every day for two weeks, I went to Sheppard Pratt from 8:30 a.m. to 3:30 p.m. going from one group therapy session to another. I saw my psychiatrist every day, except when she had to attend a 2-day conference; a nurse every morning, reporting to her how my night had gone and how my day was beginning; and I met with a social worker, who I absolutely adored. I listened to other folks' problems, cried my own tears, and cried some for them. I felt a sense of guilt from even having to be in a place like that – a mental health facility. But little by little and day by day, God showed up and strengthened me. He helped me through therapy and medication to get back up on my feet.

It has been a long but short journey in learning how to trust God in a place of brokenness and uncertainty. It has been a long but short journey in coming to grips with who I really am. It has been a long but short journey, as I watched God prove Himself to me in ways I just did not understand before. It has been a long but short journey, but I think I now know more about the God in Isaiah 45:3 (NLT) Who said, "I will give you treasures hidden in the darkness—secret riches. I will do this so you may know that I am the Lord, the God of Israel; the One who calls you by name."

But I am not the only one with a story to tell. I am not the only one who has found that "life comes at you fast." I'm not the only one who has had to tread through the hills and valleys of life. I am not the only one who has had to live life upside down while being broken into what seems like a million pieces. You have got a story too; don't you? You can testify about lost, hope, disappointment, shed tears, fiery darts, and upsetting and unsettling moments too. Can't you? Yeah, you have got a story. You can tell a story of unanswered prayers, misplaced trust, bewildering pathways, and the struggles you had trying to hold on to your sanity. I know you have got a story too, don't you? You have got a story of feeling lost and wanting desperately to be found. You have got a story of pain and tragedy and loss and despair. You have got a story of wearing the mask of how "I want to feel," instead of the real face of how "I really feel." You have got a story of grasping for straws and hoping against hope and reaching out for the unreachable. Yeah, I know you have a story too; don't you?

Yes, we've all got a story to tell because we've all been through some things and have suffered some things, but the truth of the matter is we are still here. Whatever it was, it found out it could not kill us because there is a God who will love us back to life! Whatever it was, it did not destroy our desire to keep on living! Whatever it was, it found out we would rather wait on God than give up or give in. Whatever it was, it found out we still believed in the power, providence, and purpose of God. Whatever it was, it did not break us to the point of non-repair. Whatever it was, it found out how resilient we are! Whatever it was, it found out we are not easily broken; and if we happen to break, it found out we can still fly, even if we have to do it with one wing.

Flying with One Wing is my story of being broken and finding the grace of God still available and active, even in my brokenness. It is my story of persevering in the darkest and most fearful time of my life. It is a story of pain and confusion, loneliness and desperation—a story of hope and resilience, life, and love. *Flying with One Wing* is a breath of fresh air for many who are sometimes afraid to breathe. Never despair. God's grace is always abundant and always sufficient enough for whatever we go through.

My prayer is that all who read this book will find peace, comfort, and courage for just one more day.

Pamula Yerby-Hammack
Baltimore, Maryland
September 19, 2015

INTRODUCTION

"I do not at all understand the mystery of grace—only that it meets us where we are but does not leave us where it found us."[1] I have always known about the grace of God; but I do not think I have really understood it until now, or maybe I didn't really notice it until now. I am afraid I have lived almost all of my life taking God's grace for granted. But now, I embrace God's grace and seek it every day because at any given moment on any given day, "the monster" can rise from the shadows of darkness and attack me; but God is faithful to always protect me from "the monster."

It has been over four years since "the monster" showed up to destroy my life. Even now as I write my story, "the monster" stalks me, and sometimes the remnants of anxiety's horrible breath still lurks over me. "The monster" does not want to be revealed for the monster "it" is. But I am determined to face "it" head on and reveal "its" ugliness to others by telling my story of God's grace in my time of adversity.

What I have found is God's grace is stronger than any dark, evil, force that rises up against me. His plan for my life does not stop just because my world stops. I found out my world stopped so it could start again. It stopped as I knew it so I could get off, be repaired, get back on again, and have a brand new start. I was used to living in broken places, and those broken places had become my norm. I had become comfortable in low self-worth, unhappiness, sadness, fear, and pity and had lost the ability to find my way out. I was in deep and had gotten so comfortable in the

---

[1] Quote from Anne Lamott in Max Lucado's article Why Grace is a Better Gift. http://www.churchleaders.com/pastors/pastor-articles/164439-max-lucado-why-grace-is-a-better-gift.html.

dark place that I could not see it for what it was. It was silently and slowly destroying me, and I was oblivious to its destruction.

Now with great joy, I realize I am a recipient of God's mysterious grace that met me at the mouth of that deep, dark hole of depression and anxiety. His grace did not leave me where I was, but it lovingly lifted me out of that pit and made me over again. It made me brand new. I am not the same girl I used to be. Is my wing still broken? It sure is, and I embrace it and call it mine on purpose. It is my story, and I can't deny it. I won't deny it. Why? Because I have found out that God's grace is still with me. I know that His Spirit is able to lift me higher and higher every day and cause me to live life abundantly despite my brokenness.

My brokenness does not define who I am. It does not prevent me from soaring to higher heights in Jesus. It does not keep me from being all God created me to be. In an odd way, my brokenness has become the catalyst that brings out the very best in me. Join me on my journey of discovery and adventure. Welcome to my world—my world of "flying with one wing."

Chapter One

Daddy, There's A Monster Under My Bed

"The LORD is my light and my salvation; whom
shall I fear?" Psalm 27:1 (KJV)

Allow me to share with you part of my personal story. I want to take you into my world for a brief moment and a brief look. It is early morning, Friday, September 7, 2001, possibly between 5:30 and 6:00 am. I have just awakened and made my way downstairs into my living room—a ritual I had started some time before. I am still a little sleepy and tired, but I sit as usual on my sofa. It is quiet. I am the only one awake in my house and the only light seen comes from the dim light of my curio cabinet. I settle myself and begin my quiet time with the Lord. Let me now share with you from my prayer journal entry of that memorable morning.

It's another dark morning. But then the mornings are darker when the fall season arrives. But this isn't just a darkness of the morning; there is an inner darkness here with me now. I'm not just surrounded by a darkness I can see but a darkness I can feel, as well. It's not just a darkness of the external, but it's a darkness of my spirit. I feel it. I taste it. It's been showing up every day, threatening to kill me. Its hot, foul breath is all around me. I hear its hideous laughter. It's calling me, but I won't go. It wants me I know, but I certainly don't want it. It reaches out to grab me, hold me. What is it? It's

1

ugly and horrifying. What have I done? Why does it make me a victim? Oh, I can see the inner darkness now. It's the spirit of fear and it's even more ghastly than I thought. Its mouth filled with vicious teeth has opened wide to receive its prey—ME. No! No! Get away from me. I cry. I scream. I pray. "Daddy, there's a monster under my bed." Brightness. There's brightness all around me now. Blinding, refreshing, wonderful Brightness. It has dispelled the darkness. Thank You Daddy. There was a monster under my bed, but now it's gone!

For years, and even though I did not really realize it, probably just about all of my life, I have struggled with fear. It has shown up in the most inopportune places. It has reared its ugly head in my most wonderful times and has killed my desires and dreams. Sometimes it has pressed on me and suggested I just end it all. FEAR!

I know I am not the only one who has or who continues to struggle with fear. All of us, at some point in time in our lives, have been stalked and hunted down like prey by the spirit of fear. It shows up when we least expect it, robbing us of the pleasure and joy of living. Its mission is to cast doubt in the mind and disquiet the spirit. Fear brings a darkness that is able to take our breath away. We lose all sense of joy and the will to live emotionally, mentally, spiritually, and sometimes even physically. Fear has a way of telling us "what's the use? Give up. Life is too hard for you. God doesn't care about you." And for those of us who trust Christ, fear casts shadowy doubt on His love and care for us. I would love to be able to say I have never been afraid of fear, but the truth of the matter is, there have been times when I have been petrified of it. Why...the very word fear would sometimes cause my heart to pound or keep me from even looking at the word. There have been many things I have been afraid of at some point in time in my life. I have been afraid I would lose my job. I have been afraid my loved ones would die. I have been afraid people would not like me and my friends are dissipating. I am still sometimes afraid, I will not be successful. Sometimes I am afraid I will not please Jesus. I am afraid I will have bad health. There are even times when I am afraid the trials of life will overwhelm and overtake me, and I will be destitute, alone, and left to die.

I do, however, know Someone who is not intimidated in the least by fear and its ugliness and darkness. His name is Jesus. He is the Light. He gives faith to conquer all fear. He tells me I can do all things through Him. So now when fear grips my heart and threatens to kill my desire and zest for living, especially to live for Jesus and to do His will, I will turn on the Light of Jesus Christ. I will exercise my faith, and the monster of darkness and fear will be dispelled every time. As I examine my life, I realize that my kinship with fear is not mine alone, for many people have the same propensity to fear like me and even like some of the biblical characters. One such character was a mighty warrior and king of Israel. His name was David, and he was courageous enough to write about his fears.

Tradition gives authorship of Psalm 27 to King David. According to some commentaries, there are some who believe David wrote this psalm in his younger years just as he was approaching the throne. Others believe David wrote this psalm as an aged king.[2] In any case, it was during a troublesome time for both David and his fellow Jews. Whether young or old, when David penned this Psalm he was no stranger to fear, and he was familiar with the Lord God who was able to render fear powerless.

While scholars cannot seem to agree on what occasion David wrote Psalm 27, it does seem without any contradiction that fear had been an unwelcomed companion in David's life, and there were several situations when he had to depend on the Lord for strength and courage. As someone who is also familiar with fear, I know for a fact, anxiety can show up even if there is no occasion to fear. Panic attacks often appear without warning and for no apparent reason. When anxiety would disrupt my sleep with heart palpitations, dizziness, shallow breathing, and extreme cold, I would find help in Psalm 27 when I reminded myself that the Lord Who was David's light and salvation was also mine. Over time, I learned to look fear and panic in the face and realize I had nothing to fear.

---

[2] http://www.biblestudytools.com/commentaries/matthew-henry-complete/psalms/27.html.

Chapter Two

THE DAY MY WORLD STOPPED

*"… Shall we indeed accept good from God and
not accept adversity?" Job 2:10 (NASB)*

"Falling is the only way to learn how to fly."[3] Funny, I did not know I was about to have my first lesson in how to fly. It is amazing the things we take for granted everyday—getting up out of bed, moving about freely, taking care of our personal hygiene, etc. What happens when the things you do automatically become your greatest fears? What happens when your world shifts into an eternal darkness, an unknown abyss filled with unfamiliar days and fearful nights? What happens when what used to be your life starts drifting farther and farther away from your sight until there is only the line of the horizon of where your life used to be?

On the dark, early morning of October 19, 2012, I awoke to a terrible leg cramp. I suppose the cramp had been brewing throughout the night, but there was no warning. Out of the blue, when I stretched my legs, I felt my muscle tighten. It felt as though my muscle would explode through the walls of my skin, like a volcano that would erupt. I have had leg cramps before but never like this one. I jumped out of bed and rubbed my leg, but that did not relieve the pain. I decided to try to walk it out and as I made my way to the bathroom I felt extremely nauseated. Troubling thoughts swirled around in my head as I tried to make sense out of what was going on in my body. Slowly and painfully I made my way into the small hallway outside of my bedroom. It was then that I felt an indescribable feeling as

---

[3] Proctor & Gamble Ad on YouTube 1/16/14.

though I was about to pass out. I tried to make it back to my bed so I would not fall on the floor and risk hitting my head on the small cabinet in my hallway. Everything was happening so fast though, and my ability to think could not keep up with what was happening in my body. My thoughts were all over the place—what is happening to me; I guess this is how quickly death comes. It was dark in the hallway, and I suppose my mind was getting darker and darker, too. I did manage to make it back to my bedroom, but I could stand no longer. Suddenly, I lost all control of my faculties and fell face down on the floor. It is amazing to me that I missed hitting my head on my dresser! But as I look back now, I realize God's perfect promises are always in effect. Psalm 91:11-12 NIV says, "For He will command His angels concerning you to guard you in all your ways; they will lift you up in their hands so that you will not strike your foot against a stone." I could not see them, but I know for a fact God's angels were right there with me.

Thank God, my husband Van was home. When he heard me fall, he came to my rescue. I could tell he was just as bewildered as I was. I could hear it in his voice as he asked me what happened. "What happened?" I didn't have the slightest clue. So, I did not have an answer for him. I was still asking myself the same question. Nothing like that had ever happened to me before. I am in good physical health. But from out of nowhere, something overtook my body, and before I knew it, I was on the floor feeling my husband's strong but gentle arms turning me over and lifting me up. That is when I realized my life had drastically changed. When I went to bed, I was fine, or so I thought. But somewhere between the time I laid down to sleep and the time I was awakened by the leg cramp, something unknown had crept into my world to turn it upside down. At that moment in time, it was still unclear to me why my world was so drastically altered because of a simple leg cramp. As I said before, leg cramps are nothing new to me. I have had them before; but along with the physical pain of this leg cramp, apparently there was also a spiritual attack. Out of the shadows of the darkness of that morning, something even darker had risen to intimidate me. I am not scheduled to work on Fridays (that definitely worked to my advantage on that day), and I usually plan to sleep a little longer than I do on other days of the week. However, not on this Friday. My unplanned and unfamiliar awakening would not allow me to comfortably return back to bed and to sleep. How could I? I could not risk facing another episode. As a matter of fact, I thought it best just to lie in bed and not move at all. I thought lying in bed was the safest place for me—still, unmoving and quiet. Yep, that is exactly how to play it safe.

Medical tests would prove physically I was fine, but spiritually and mentally something was terribly wrong. When my husband picked me up from off the floor, I had no idea my life had taken a turn in the road. All I knew was suddenly and without warning, I was plunged into a world of darkness, fear, confusion, and panic.

In the Old Testament Book of Job, we read about a man's story of sudden destruction, loss, grief, and uncertainty. I cannot help but wonder if Job felt anything like I did on that dark October 19th morning. In chapter one of the book that bears his name, we are introduced to this man Job who is described by God as "a blameless and upright man, fearing God and turning away from evil." God said there was "no one like him on the earth."[4] Wow! What a man Job must have been. Can you imagine our perfect God saying that about you? I know I can't. I am more like the Apostle Paul when he said, "For I know that nothing good dwells in me, that is, in my flesh…"(Romans 7:18 NASB). However, there is hope; but I will talk about that a little later on.

Job found himself the victim of one calamity after another. He lost his family. He lost his wealth. He lost his health. In a matter of minutes and without any warning, Job's life was completely changed, like mine—different situations but the same outcome. We both had been thrust into a place of uncertainty.

Have you ever stopped to ask yourself, "Where in the world is God when my life has been turned upside down? Does He even hear my cries for help? Does He even care?" I cannot help but wonder why He did not stop my life from being altered. It would be understandable if things were the other way around. If my life was already in a mess and God allowed something drastic to turn it around in a good way, I would understand that change. But what about when my life is going smoothly and God allows something drastic to turn my life in a bad direction? That is incomprehensible.

---

[4] Job 1:8 (NASB)

I am amazed that after all the tragic things that happened to Job, he was still faithful enough to God to accept what God allowed. Instead of blaming God, cursing God, or turning against God, Job humbly submitted to God's sovereignty and asked the profound question, "Shall we indeed accept good from God and not accept adversity?"[5] How could Job peer past the pain and calamity that quickly permeated his life and still trust God? When one servant after the other paraded in front of him to deliver yet another bad report, how could Job find it in his heart to trust in God's providence? I don't know. All I know is that it took a long time for me to even mention the words October 19, without feeling anxious or fearful. It was a dark day for me, and like Job (Job 3:3), I wish it could be erased out of my life; but I know it will not. It will forever be etched in time and in eternity as the day my world stopped!

---

[5] Job 2:10b

Chapter Three

LIFE IN THE VALLEY OF DARKNESS

"Even when I walk through the darkest valley, I will not be afraid, for you are close beside me." Psalm 23:4 (NLT)

I spent the entire day in bed. My daughter, Cianni, came over after work and sat with me until midnight. She fed me, talked with me, and gave me medicine to help me sleep. After she tucked me in, she stayed about another forty-five minutes talking to her father. I am sure the events of the day were the topic of their conversation.

On the day after my fall, I woke up around 5:30 a.m. (totally out of the norm since it was a Saturday morning). My hands were white, my lips were a little pale, and my leg still hurt from where the cramp had been. I was cold and weak, but I felt better than I had felt the day before. I wanted so badly to climb back in the bed, but I knew I had other responsibilities that day and that was not possible. I made my way downstairs (without falling this time, praise the Lord) to the living room to sit in my favorite chair to journal my prayers to the Lord. My hands were shaking, and it was hard for me to write; but I spent the next forty minutes revealing my heart to God in writing. I told God I had laid in bed all day the day before and about how queasy my stomach had been. I had not been able to even get up to eat and take care of my personal hygiene, but my daughter saw to it that I had everything I needed. I told God how thankful I was to have her and my husband attending to me.

I wrote, "Oh Lord, I need Your help! Something is wrong and I need Your help!" Despite my weakness and confusion, the Lord gave me strength to teach a workshop for the women at Wayside Baptist Church that afternoon. I guess if I was not so full of anxiety, I might have laughed at the irony of it all because the workshop was the second part of a series I taught at the same church on fear and faith prior to me becoming consumed with my own fears. I was living now what I had previously taught. I felt like everyone could see something was wrong, but not so. I thought I looked weak and frail, but God had somehow veiled my appearance and no one was the wiser. Sometimes I alternate sitting and standing when I teach, but that day I had to sit through the entire teaching. I had no strength to stand. It was all I could do just to be there. I love teaching God's Word, and I especially love teaching women about the God Who loves them so much. But on this day, I was so glad when the teaching was over and Cianni could whisk me away and take me back home to crawl into the safe haven of my bed. I was ready to go back into the dark hole I had been living in. I did not feel like I needed to go to the hospital on the day of the fall, but Cianni and Van convinced me to make an appointment with my primary care doctor for that upcoming Monday.

Well, Monday arrived and I still could not seem to shake the cold feeling I had. My legs shook because they felt cold, yet I knew the weather was not cold at all. The day was sunny and bright and the temperature range, according to the CME U.S. Weekly Temperature File for Monday, October 22, 2012, would have been between 43 and 71 degrees,[6] certainly not really cold yet for Baltimore. I would later learn that the coldness I felt was the chilliness of FEAR. We arrived at Dr. Khan's office. Cianni and I sat in chairs near the front door while Van checked me in. Dr. Khan has been my primary care doctor for at least sixteen years. I see him on a regular basis, and he and his staff know me well. They know my personality and my demeanor. But on this day when I walked into the office, Dr. Khan and his staff were mystified as to what had happened to me. I know they were because they kept asking my husband and daughter, "What happened to her?" I usually show up bright and chipper, but not on this day. I was fearful and withdrawn. From my perspective, they were looking at me as if they had seen a ghost. I know that was not true, but I also knew my behavior was totally out of character for me.

---

[6] ftp://ftp.cmegroup.com/weather/usa/temperature/weekly/USA_Weekly October_22_2012.pdf.

Waiting to be seen was difficult, but I tried to have courage. I sat close to my daughter and shared a song on my iPod I had listened to the night before that gave me comfort. While we were sharing the ear plugs and enjoying the music, an odd thing happened. The front door opened and in walked a woman with a bubbly personality. When I turned to see who was coming through the door, she looked directly at me as if she was looking for me. Her clear and pleasant eyes appeared to look deep into my pain. After she signed in she came right over to me, looked me straight in the eye with a warm, loving, smile on her face and asked, "What's wrong mama?" How did she even know I was somebody's mother? I do not believe Cianni and I gave her any indication we were mother and daughter. It was obvious we knew each other, but other than that, how did she know? I told her I had been better, and then she shared some things about her and her daughter. She was very talkative and my husband was annoyed by her constant talking. I was not. Actually, she had a calming presence about her, and she was very pleasant. The stories she shared helped me in some small way to let go of the mental pain I was in. I truly believe the Lord sent this lady to sit with me to help ease the tension and the anxiety I was experiencing.[7] The Bible tells us to entertain strangers with hospitality because we could be entertaining angels without knowing it.[8] Was this woman an angel? I do not know for sure, but I do know she was sent just for me. To those in the doctor's office she was just another patient, but to me she was an angel of comfort sent by my loving God.

After what seemed like a long time, I was finally called back into one of the small clinic rooms. Nervously, I followed the nurse, and my husband and daughter followed me. The nurse, still puzzled by my appearance, asked again what had happened to me. Then, with a look of concern she wished me well.

Dr. Kahn was confused when he saw me. He had never seen me like that before, and I had never been like that before. As a physician, he is used to seeing "sick" people, but I do not think I presented myself as someone who was "sick." I just looked confused and off-track. It was hard for me to talk about what had happened, but my husband and daughter were able to help explain the events that brought me to his office on that day. Dr. Kahn

---

[7] The next day in my journal I thanked the Lord for sending this woman to me.
[8] Hebrews 13:2

took my vital signs and everything was fine—blood pressure good, pulse good, lungs clear, and heat beat in perfect rhythm with only the normal benign murmur detected. The only thing he could conclude was perhaps I had a sudden drop in blood pressure because of the painful leg cramp and that is what caused me to fall. Dr. Kahn was pretty certain I didn't have a blood clot, stating, it would have already traveled to my lungs since the incident happened four days ago. However, a mysterious bruise on my left leg, above where I had had the cramp, caused Dr. Khan to order a Doppler test. Oh, I was so afraid. What if there was a clot? What would that mean? I did not want to take that test and had actually feared taking this test for quite some time.

Perhaps I should pause here to attempt to explain my fear of being ill. From a child, I had always been blessed with good health. I did not even have my first hospital stay until I was forty years of age. When I entered my fifties, age and genetic-related problems began to show up— hypertension, high cholesterol, and being overweight. With these medical issues, I was introduced to a world of more frequent doctor's visits and medications. It definitely was not something I was used to, since all my life I had experienced great health. In addition, I was also privileged to live in a family that had enjoyed great health. Hospitals, doctors, and medications were not a frequent part of our story. But my story drastically changed when my husband and I were married. Unfortunately, before we celebrated our first-year anniversary, my husband started having serious health problems that plagued him throughout the rest of his life and our marriage.

I believe I began to internalize my husband's health problems, so much so, I unconsciously made them mine. Having to deal with Van's hospital visits and stays, which included watching him go through pain, sitting in the waiting area while he went through yet another procedure, staying by his bedside when he was admitted, and just taking care of him during his severe health challenges, caused Van's health problems to ultimately seep into my subconscious and become mine. Among other things, my husband had heart disease; so, I especially became very fearful of having a heart attack. I know I had real health issues, but the truth is I kept up with my doctor's appointments, took my medications properly, and tried to eat healthy. My husband, on the other hand, did not follow his doctor's orders as he should have. This led to frequent hospital visits and his deteriorating health. Why then should I expect to have the same health problems as he did? What was going on in my mind? With every emergency room visit with my husband, my fear was just as much for myself as it was for him. Of course, I did not mention my fear to anyone. I was a bit superstitious, thinking that if I said the words "heart attack" out loud, it would cause me to have one. Having unhealthy empathy for my husband, only intensified my own fears concerning my health. Over the years, my fear of being sick would not improve as long as Van continued to experience bad health.

Getting back to the Doppler—even though I was fearful of having the test done, I followed Dr. Kahn's advice. His nurse scheduled a stat appointment at the radiology facility. What a difference a day makes. Thursday past, I was fine—going through life as usual. Friday morning, everything changed. There I was waiting to have tests done to see if I had a blood clot. My anxiety rose tremendously!

I was definitely too afraid to go into the dark room to have the test done without my trusty "security blanket", Cianni. She patiently and lovingly followed me into the room. Cianni was very happy the test had been scheduled because she was afraid I had a blood clot. By God's grace and mercy, I was able to have the test and was comforted by the technician. She could see no evidence of clots! I would, however, have to wait for the full report. That was good news, but my anxiety would not let me be comforted. I could not get past the "what ifs." My mind immediately began to think, "What if this young lady does not know what she is doing? What if there is a mistake in the report? What if one thing and what if another thing?" Why wouldn't my thoughts let me find comfort in what I was told? Why couldn't I believe what the professionals were saying? I was so glad to leave, not necessarily because I was blessed to receive a good report, but because I just wanted to get out of there and run back home to my place of safety—my nice, comfortable, safe bed. What a day! What a day! What a very, very hard day!

I lived in a fog of fear, panic, confusion, and a struggle with my faith in God for weeks. I was not able to pray (or so I thought), to write, or to concentrate on reading His Word. I could not work. I could not continue school. I could not take care of my housework. I could not even take care of myself. What had happened to me? Had I done something wrong? Was this an attack of the devil, or was this something sent by God—a thorn in my side maybe to humble me and to teach me valuable lessons I had not yet learned? Whatever it was, I did not like it. Wherever it came from, I wanted it to go back.

Every day was different. Some days were easier than others. The fog came and went. One day, I could walk without feeling like I would fall; and the next day, I stumbled along not being able to handle life alone. The anxiety attacks continued, and they left me weak and afraid, feeling isolated from the rest of the world and alone. I was a complete mess! I prayed God would have mercy on me.

With that one fall, I had been thrown into a desolate and unknown world. I knew I did not belong there. I was not a citizen and I desperately wanted to escape. I was being held captive against my will by some strange and evil force. Familiar became unfamiliar. Light became dark. Smiles were overcome with tears. I struggled to find truth amidst the lies.

It was awful having to live with "the monster." For example, the shower became a place of terror and threatening. I do not know why. All I know is that I could not take a shower. The soothing and refreshing droplets of my personal rainforest had suddenly become a prison that held me captive. The shower no longer embraced me; it attacked me. My shower, any shower for that matter, was no longer a sanctuary of peace and tranquility. It was a chamber of horrors. The droplets of water had teeth to destroy me. Being alone behind a curtain where no one could see me was threatening. For the days after my fall, I did not dare take a shower. I knew it was necessary to take care of my personal hygiene. So, I resorted to taking baths. But only if Van or Cianni were there to watch me, and then it had to be quick. I could not stay in the bathtub for long because of the fear it held for me.

For weeks, I sought help from the medical and psychiatric community, only to have every door shut in my face. Meanwhile, family and friends tried helping me by reminding me to trust in God or by quoting Scriptures. They also tried helping by encouraging me to do things that were necessary and familiar but had become more fearful to me than anything I had ever experienced. I began to feel isolated from family and friends and even strangers on the street as I watched everybody living their lives and going on as if nothing had happened to me. I was lost. I was lonely. I was on an island all by myself with nobody to care. Thoughts swirled in my head that may not have been true or made sense, but they were my thoughts. I lived each day with the fear I would lose all my faculties again and fall.

My bed, my home, were no longer places of comfort. I had to find another comfort place—my daughter, Cianni's house. But because many felt I was not doing things on my own, but rather being babied and pampered, and therefore not getting any better, I was taken from that comfort place, and moved to my baby sister's house with her and her husband. This became my new place of comfort. (At some point in my journey, I did return home with my husband). I'm grateful for all those who extended an open door to me, but because of fear, change was hard.

In my mind, the truth was nobody really knew what was wrong, and nobody really knew how to help me, except a few who had experienced firsthand what I was going through and my daughter who refused to allow this monster to get the best of me.

It is difficult to walk through the dark valley of mental illness; but it may be more difficult for the family, friends, and outsiders who have to walk it with you. In my own twisted thinking, senseless things made sense. But how can you explain to someone else the intense, paralyzing, and debilitating fear you have of taking your morning shower or walking into the Rite Aid Pharmacy or the Toys R Us store? How can you explain to someone else your fear of sitting on the toilet because once when you did, your entire body started to tingle, and you thought you were having a stroke? How can you expect someone else to fully understand your irrational thinking in being determined to go to work in the middle of a hurricane? Ah yes, the hurricane experience.

It was said, "Hurricane Sandy was the deadliest and most destructive hurricane of the 2012 Atlantic hurricane season."[9] By the time it reached us, the news called it "Super Storm Sandy." It was still quite powerful! But regardless of the storm that was brewing outside, fear of being absent from my job for too many days because of my illness drove me to try to get to work. My thinking is much clearer now. What made perfectly good sense to me on that dark, rainy, windy, Monday morning, October 29, 2012, I now see as ridiculous and dangerous. After receiving help from the Lord through His Word and the professionals He sent to help get me through

---

[9] http://en.wikipedia.org/wiki/Hurricane_Sandy. Last modified on 29 September 2013 at 23:45.

that nightmarish existence, the events of that day are even hilarious to me now. But back then, it was not funny. It was real and something I had to do. Did I know it was a dangerous storm? Absolutely!

Days before, the newscasters gave detailed descriptions of the magnitude of the storm that was headed our way. I knew it was slated as monstrous. I knew it was not to be trivialized. I watched the news on the big screen television while sitting on the loveseat in my mom and dad's comfortable family room. I even mentioned it in a sermon the Sunday before the storm burst through the doorway of our city. Yet, somehow on that Monday morning, I lost all sense of the warnings that had come my way. I proceeded to make my way through the storm. No one could stop me. Pleadings from my mother were futile. Warnings from my father were dismissed. I had to go to work!

As I left Mommy and Daddy's house and made my way through the darkness, through the wind, and through the rain to my little red SUV, I had no idea it would be over a month before I sat behind the wheel to drive again. I still did not know what was wrong with me. All I knew was fear had become a constant companion. I did not want it, but I could not get rid of it either. I gingerly walked to the SUV with the rain beating upon me, put my things on the back seat, and snuggled up under the steering wheel. "Whew! I made it!" I had made plans to pick up my coworker (a very dear girlfriend) who was staying nearby. I did not exactly know where I was going, and the darkness was a hindrance; but I pressed on. Finally, I found her and she got in the car. She had no idea what I was going through, and she probably could not see my face very well in the darkness.

We finally arrived at our workplace. As soon as I got out of the vehicle, grabbed my things, and started to walk, I was immediately thrown into a wave of anxiety. Fear overtook me, and I could not walk. It was as though an invisible shield was put up in front of me to keep me from moving forward or as if sudden paralysis had taken over my body. I was stiffened by the fear and felt weak under its grasp. I was so glad I was not alone. Being the good friend, and sister she is, Fee grabbed me by the arm and carefully and lovingly escorted me to the front door of our workplace. The rain was horrendous. The wind was turbulent. I was still unable to maneuver by myself, so Fee led me to a chair in the lobby to wait for her while she put her things in her office. I have walked confidently through that lobby so many times, but this time I was surrounded by fear and did not want to be there. "Hurry, Fee! Hurry!"

I know the guard who I usually smile at and speak to was probably wondering what was going on with me. I could see it in her eyes. After what seemed like an eternity, Fee returned, took me by the arm, and escorted me to the building I work in.

Up the elevator we went and down the hallway that led to the front door. Rain was pouring, winds were blowing, and the street was practically empty. Why? It was Monday morning. A work day. Where was everybody? I do not know what was going through Fee's mind. But I knew by then, she had to know something was not right with me. Do you remember the tornado in the Wizard of Oz that whipped through Kansas and snatched up Dorothy and her house? I think that was how I was feeling—like any minute, I would be whisked away in the storm. It would have been easy because I did not weigh much at the time. Our coats were blowing. We struggled to keep our umbrellas from turning inside out. The wind and the rain had no mercy on two women almost alone in the storm trying to make their way. I suppose it still did not seem odd to me that the only people I saw at work were the security guards. I thought it was just probably because the storm had slowed everybody up. I was shaking from fear and feeling weak as Fee and I entered through the front door of my building, took the elevator up to the third floor, and walked into my office. It was after I got in the office, turned on the light, and sat down that Fee got a real, good look at me. She knew something was terribly wrong. What did she see? Did she see horror? Did she see emptiness? What was it? Whatever it was, it prompted her to pray to the Lord God for help. She anointed my office with oil and prayed fervently for the Lord to make haste to help her friend. She knew her sister friend was in deep trouble and needed help NOW!

I was amazed at what happened next, and if I weren't so fearful, I would have burst out laughing. I logged into my computer and checked my emails, just to discover the institute was closed for the day because of the weather! Only essential employees were required to come to work. Oh no! After plowing through the storm, I now had to go right back home. If I had been my normal self, I would have squealed with delight to get a day off; however, I was not my normal self. That is why I was there in the first place, in the middle of the "storm of the year!" I was afraid to drive back home. Fee had already gone back across the street to her office, so I called her and gave her the news that we didn't even have to come to work. We were in a dilemma. Fee does not drive in storms and now I was afraid to drive, period! Both of us were afraid! How would I get home? What's a girl to do? I called Cianni and told her my problem; and once more, she came to my rescue. Cianni and my darling son-in-love, TC, showed up as quickly as they could. Then Cianni drove me to my mom and dad's house while TC drove my car.

Mental illness does not involve just you. Everyone is affected by your irrational thinking and poor judgment and decisions. Therefore, you need good friends and loving family members as you walk through the dark valley of mental illness. You need people who are patient with you. You need people who are not judgmental, but rather compassionate and willing to stand by your side no matter how irrational your behavior. You need people who know the real you and who will not cast you aside when you offend them or lash out at them for no reason at all. Thank God for friends like Fee and Dana (another sister, friend). Thank God for loving and caring family members like my husband, my parents, my children, and my siblings.

"Oh Father, when will this TORMENT end? I am tormented day and night. FEAR and DREAD have become my daily partners. They seek to overcome me. They seek to take my life. But Jesus said He had come to give me abundant life (John 10:10). I long for peace of mind and rest in my spirit. I long for stability and joy. I long for deliverance and wholeness. How long, my Father, must I suffer? How long must I struggle? How long will I have to be in this dark pit of despair, this lonely island of exile, this abandoned shack of fear? HOW LONG ABBA?"[10]

Panic and fear are terrible to live with. If I never have another panic attack in my life, it will not be too soon. I suppose my first realized panic attack came on while sitting in my baby sister's kitchen.[11] I was trying to do work on the laptop when out of nowhere an overwhelming sense of fear overtook me. My sister had been in the kitchen with me, but she left me

---

[10] From my journal: Tuesday, November 13, 2012 @ 6:14am in my baby sister's kitchen.

[11] I had gone from living at home, living with my parents, living with my daughter, and now living with my baby sister Lisa.

and I was alone. I could not be left alone. I was too afraid to be alone. The panic escalated higher and higher when I could not find my sister in the house, and I could not breathe. I was too afraid to get up out of the chair, but I knew I couldn't just sit there and die. So, against all fear, I made my way to the door to get air and find my sister. "Lisa! Lisa! Where are you?" No answer. Where was she? How could she leave me in this big house all alone? "Lisa!" I called. "Lisa!" She was nowhere to be found. I made my way to the front door trying to catch my breath and look for my sister. Louder and louder I called, "Lisa!" Still no answer. The panic rose higher. Just as I was about to lose my mind, my sister came up from downstairs. She could see the panic and asked what was wrong. With tears in my eyes, I had to confess when I could not find her, I panicked. The panic finally subsided when I saw her.

Another terrible panic attack came on after I had been prescribed Zoloft (Sertraline). Dr. Kahn said it was a trusted medicine used to treat anxiety and gave me a dosage of 50 mg. Though I was afraid to take the medication,[12] I trusted Dr. Khan. I came home, took the medicine, and laid down. I dozed right off into a deep sleep. But around 9:00 pm that evening, I awoke to a pounding heart, chills, and trouble breathing. Thank God Van and Cianni were near. I am not one to run to doctors and emergency rooms, but on that night, I pleaded for them to take me quick and in a hurry. Something was horribly wrong. I had never felt like that before. I do not remember the drive to the emergency room, but I do remember arriving there. I was immediately taken into the triage room and given an EKG. It seemed unbelievable, but the EKG was normal. That doesn't seem possible since my heart was racing and about to come out of my chest! The lab test revealed a drop in my potassium level, which my daughter believed was a result of my not eating. She believed this sudden drop in potassium, along with the high dosage of Zoloft, produced the unpleasant heart palpitations.

Oddly enough, I do not remember feeling nervous either. Why? My body was certainly in distress. Maybe it was because I just wanted somebody to help me. By God's grace and mercy, my heart eventually

---

[12] I don't like taking medicine of any kind. I dreaded having to take yet another pill! And besides this others had warned me against taking medications that are prescribed for mental health issues.

calmed down from a high-speed gallop to its normal purr and my breathing was stabilized. The doctor performed a brief examination and assured me I was okay medically, but highly recommended I seek a psychiatric evaluation. He administered a small dose of Klonopin (Clonazepam) to help me stay calm and a dose of potassium to bring my levels back within normal range. The doctor gave me an option of staying the night in the hospital for observation or going home. I wasn't sure what I should do. I was feeling better, but I just could not be sure. Let me add, my daughter is a medical technician; thus, she has a good working knowledge of medicine. She is also intelligent, wise, godly, and a woman of prayer. Cianni has always helped my husband and I make good decisions about our health, so I trust her completely. I had become very dependent upon her for everything and was afraid to make any decisions without her. I turned to my daughter and asked her opinion, but she left the decision up to me. I still did not trust what might happen, so I asked her if she thought I was okay enough to leave. She thought I was fine to go home, and I trusted her. Since the test results showed there was nothing physically wrong with me, since I was feeling much calmer, and since my daughter thought I was fine, I decided against staying overnight at the hospital. However, I had a problem. I did not want to go back to my house. Just thinking about going back there caused the anxiety to grip me like a tight, fitting glove, and I became very agitated at the very thought of returning home.

Clearly in my mind, this panic attack was drug-induced. I knew I should not have taken that pill in the first place. No more of that drug for me! Because of this experience, I did not want to be given any medications for fear the same thing might happen again. It was the monster! Fear caused this. I felt like I had taken a journey through the valley of the shadow of death, and I was about to be consumed by it. Is this what the psalmist, David, was describing in Psalm 23:4?

Warren Wievsrsbe in his book, *Be Worshipful*[13] writes, "While people of all ages love and quote this Psalm, its message is for mature Christians who have fought battles and carried burdens." I was definitely in a battle, and carrying a heavy burden. Surely, Psalm 23 had the instructions I needed to fight and the encouragement I needed to endure.

---

[13] Psalm 23. http://theapprovedworkman.blogspot.com/2006/04/psalm-23-introduction.html.

It seems quite appropriate to me that David would liken God to a shepherd since before becoming king of Israel, he was a shepherd tending his father's flock. As a shepherd, he could understand what it meant to care for, nurture, guide, and protect those who were weak and helpless. As David tended the flock, he also became quite familiar with the dangers present in the wilderness (valley). His life was endangered by bears and lions.[14] Yet, as David led the sheep through the valley and feared the reality of the possibility of death, he was comforted by the fact that God was with him every step of the way. The fear of evil was diminished as he remembered the Shepherd of his soul. Death was merely a shadow hovering over him. He knew, just as I knew, shadows cannot hurt you.

It has been noted that the Psalm begins and ends with "The Lord."[15] By doing this, the Psalm picks up the theme found in Revelation 1:8, where Jesus said, "I am Alpha and Omega, the beginning and the ending" (KJV). An unspoken thought in this verse is "Jesus is also in between". One would think that this would give me hope knowing the Lord stood at the beginning of my hard trial; He would even stand in the middle of my trial, and He would remain standing until the end of it. However, fear had trumped my faith. I couldn't really be sure I could rest in this promise.

Could I confidently walk with God in the dark valley of fear like David? Or, would fear loom large over me with its glistening teeth and foul breath? Oh God, take me through this darkness and do not ever leave me.

---

[14] "But David said to Saul, 'your servant has been keeping his father's sheep. When a lion or a bear came and carried off a sheep from the flock, I went after it...'" (I Samuel 17:34-35 NIV)

[15] Psalm 23. http://theapprovedworkman.blogspot.com/2006/04/psalm-23-introduction.html.

Chapter Four

BABY STEPS

"Though I walk in the midst of trouble, Thou wilt revive me." Psalm 138:7a (KJV)

I love watching babies take their first steps. Step. Step. Wobble. Wobble. Eventually, they get it right or they just resort to crawling along a little longer. I never thought at the age of fifty-seven I would have to learn to walk (with confidence that is) all over again. But after my fall, I became afraid to walk for fear it would happen again. My confident and swift footsteps became unsure and slow. Step. Step. Wobble. Wobble. Like a baby learning to walk, I lacked the confidence to stride; and instead, I either shuffled along or took small steps.

Funny, I soon learned the key to gaining my confidence back would be found in taking "baby steps," moving toward health and wholeness one step at a time. Step. Step. Wobble. Wobble. I could no longer live my life with things piling up on each other. I could no longer allow my days and my nights to become one entity; I had to learn to separate the two. I could not "keep running on empty." But I realized I had to allow my body and my mind to recuperate and refresh in order to be revived and rejuvenated. I also knew I could not do it alone. I longed for somebody to help me. I had fallen, and I did not know how to get back up. I needed somebody to show me the way up, the way out, and the way through this maze of darkness and confusion.

My first attempt to find someone to help me in the mental health field came on the heels of an especially painful time of feeling isolated. I was staying with my daughter at the time and an overwhelming sense of being disconnected from the rest of the world came over me. I do not believe I have ever felt so alone in my life. I knew there were people around me and they were willing to help me, but I still could not shake the extreme sense of loneliness. The sadness was overwhelming. Somehow it came to me to call Fee and ask for help. She recommended a social worker she thought may have been able to help me. Fortunately, the social worker was willing to see me. Ironically, her office was not far from where I lived. My baby sister took me to my first appointment and dropped me off. I never knew walking into a building, getting on an elevator, and walking down a hallway could be so frightening. I staggered down the long hallway holding onto the wall. I thought I would never make it. At long last, I made it to Dr. Ford-Edwards's office. She was a pleasant, attractive woman with an inviting smile. She patiently listened to me tell my story and quickly recognized my need for mental health treatment. She believed I was in need of medication; however, she could not prescribe it. I had to see a psychiatrist for any medication I may have needed. Then she asked me the oddest question, "What games did you like to play as a child?" What did that have to do with anything? That was a long time ago anyway, and I did not see how that would help anything now. But I told tell her I enjoyed playing the game of jacks. My assignment was simple. Bring some jacks with me the next week and we were going to play. I came the following week with my jacks, and we played a game or two. I must admit, it did make me feel a little bit lighter. She explained I had been so busy filling my life up with work—at the workplace, in ministry, and at home that I had forgotten how to play. I suppose there is something to be said about the old adage, "All work and no play makes Jack a dull boy." Except, I did not become bored from so much work. Instead, I had become depressed and fearful. Dr. Ford-Edwards taught me a valuable lesson about taking time to enjoy life. Unfortunately, Dr. Ford-Edwards knew I needed intensive help she was not qualified to give, and my search for help continued.

I thought I had found the help I needed when I went to see a workplace counselor. I did not go to the appointment alone because I couldn't. My anxiety would not allow it. It haunted me every second of every day and made it impossible for me to do anything alone. Also, the anxiety would not allow me to trust my family. I only felt safe with one person, my daughter Cianni; and I did not dare go anywhere, nor do anything without her. She was the only one I could trust. I do not know why, but I felt so vulnerable and so frightened without her. On one hand, I felt terrible for putting such pressure on her to accompany me everywhere; but on the other hand, I thought, how would I be able to live without her?

I was happy to tell a mental health professional about all I was going through. My daughter left the office, and nervously I followed the counselor into a room off of the waiting area. I sat on a couch, and he sat a short distance across the room from me. I could hardly speak without crying. As I talked about my fear and the other problems in my life, tears flowed like water in a babbling brook. Here I was baring my soul to a complete stranger. I know he was listening, but did he really care? What was going through his mind? After listening to my story, he said he was not the appropriate person for me to see, and suggested it would be best if I saw a psychiatrist. Something about medication was also mentioned. Finally, somebody agreed with me! However, he did not give me a referral. What was I supposed to do now? Where was I supposed to go? Was this appointment just a waste of my time? The session lasted an hour, and the only thing I had from my visit was a date to come see him again. When I left that office, I had nothing more to go on than when I arrived. *Sigh!*

My next appointment with the workplace counselor was the following week. I entered the office with hopes he would refer me to a psychiatrist or psychologist but he did not. The counselor gave me a few options, instead. First, he suggested I could continue to see Dr. Ford-Edwards. He thought she was a good match for me, especially since she was a Christian minister as well. Secondly, he suggested I search the website of my insurance company for names of psychiatrists. I was confused and upset! Really? Was that all he had to offer me? I could not concentrate. I was scared out of my wits, and he was sending me to the Internet? *Sigh!* His next suggestion was, I could ask my primary care physician to prescribe anti-anxiety medication for me. Lastly, he said he would email me a list of two or three therapists to address my issues; although by the way, he was not sure when he would be able to do it. By now, it seemed clear to me I was a low priority. I left his office feeling defeated. "God, where is the help I need?"[16]

---

[16] From my prayer journal: "Holy Spirit, please guide me and lead me. I don't know what to do or where to turn. I really, really need you" 11/14/12.

The help I longed for came on November 21, 2012, one day before Thanksgiving. It had been over a month and I was still trying to get over my fears and sadness. Although I had the help of well-meaning family and friends, I knew deep down inside I needed more. It wasn't that people were not praying for me. As a matter of fact, one faithful friend, Maxine, texted me a prayer every morning at 5:00 am—the time I would normally awake (if I had been asleep at all). She even fasted for me. I knew my parents, husband, daughter, siblings, and other friends were all praying for me. They were deeply concerned, but I was not getting any better. Rather, I was sinking deeper and deeper in the pit of despair and fear.[17] I did not want to sink deeper. I needed help, and I needed it right away! I felt like I needed psychiatric help.

Because my mind was not clear at that time, there is so much about "the day I went to get help," I cannot remember. My daughter had to fill in many of the blanks for me. She said she vowed never to go down that painful road again, but she did because I needed to know what it was like—what I was like.

The day following my visit to the ER, I am sure I was still tired from the events of the evening and reeling from the harrowing experience of the panic attack. Panic attacks are surely no fun, and besides the fear, they can leave you drained. My husband had to go to work, which meant Cianni had to come over to take care of me and sit with me. After she helped me bathe, we looked for a list of professional phone numbers which were given to me to help me locate a mental health provider. Perhaps my trip to the workplace counselor yielded something after all, but I found out my husband had taken the list with him to work. I suppose he was going to try to find someone to help me. I do not know. But when we discovered the list was not at the house, we knew all we could do was wait until my husband returned. Unfortunately, the wait was very unpleasant for me. My anguish grew deeper and stronger. I am going to step back now and let Cianni speak for herself of what she saw when she looked at me.

"At one glance you appeared like a wet noodle barely capable of standing in your own strength (Me: I don't really think I had any strength).

---

[17] This reminds me of the woman with the issue of blood in Mark 5:25-34. She spent 12 years trying to find a cure for her bleeding and instead of getting better she only got worse. Thank God I didn't have to wait for 12 years to find help!

Your shoulders were far from squared. In fact, they were rounded forward and your clothes hung on you. Everything about your frame screamed out unhappiness and you had a sad demeanor."

It was at that point Cianni grew frustrated and was provoked to move on my behalf because she felt like something really needed to be done, and it had to be done immediately.

Cianni began searching for mental health professionals who could offer me help through means of traditional medicine and/or holistic. I joined her in the search, offering what little help I could. Can I just say that surfing the Internet with its vast amount of entries is tiring and disheartening when you cannot concentrate and you do not have a clue as to what you are looking for! In my opinion, to give someone who cannot function in the basic day-to-day activities of life a list of names and advise them to "go fish" for their own help is both unprofessional and uncaring. I am not trying to discredit the counselor I saw. I am sure he is very good at what he does, but I am saying he did not give *me* much hope. Thank God I had family and friends who would go the extra mile with me. I pray[18] for those who are struggling with mental illness and have nowhere to turn.

In the meantime, my husband returned home with the sad news that he had been unsuccessful in trying to reach anyone to help me. I am going to let Cianni speak again.

"You sank a little more with each passing moment. You were pacing the floor as your eyes continued to water with tears. Occasionally, you would rest your hands on your head in discomfort. You constantly said, 'I need to talk to somebody.'"

No longer willing to wait for my husband to reach somebody or to wait for phone calls to be returned, Cianni decided to call my insurance company. My husband, who really was not fond of the idea of me seeking help from mental health professionals, became very demanding. He began requesting the list of phone numbers given to my daughter while she was on the phone in the middle of a conversation with a representative. That was distracting, but Cianni continued on her quest to get her mother the help she needed. Initially, the call was the same as we had heard before;

---

[18] Dear Lord, I pray for those who are all alone in their struggles. Draw near to them and help them. I thank You that Your word says we can cast all our anxieties on You because You care for us (1 Peter 5:7). In Jesus' name. Amen.

"Take two pills and call me in the morning." Yes, I am being sarcastic. That is to say, we were given another list of phone numbers to doctors' offices. This was a very tense time for all of us, as my weak mental state threatened to take everyone around me captive. But Cianni can be very persuasive, and she knows how to get what she needs. She politely thanked the person on the other end of the phone, and proceeded to tell her she believed I was in a crisis situation. She reminded the representative it was Thanksgiving weekend, and we had been unsuccessful in contacting a provider. The representative replied with two words that would be critical to my wellness. She suggested "Sheppard Pratt". If I weren't so sad, perhaps I would have erupted into a jovial dance of merriment. But alas, my tearful and somber state would not allow me any joy. *Sigh*.

Nevertheless, that one phone call pointed us in the right direction. It was the beginning of the "yellow brick road" that would lead me to the land of freedom!

My daughter told me while she was trying to find me help, I got very flustered. In my agitation I said, "I can't take this any longer! I have got to go somewhere to get help!" While she talked to me in a calm demeanor to try and tell me what the representative said, my husband abruptly interjected once more with his disapproval of Sheppard Pratt. Why is everyone so afraid of mental illness? Why is it so hard to understand if your lungs can be sick, or your heart can be sick, or your kidneys can be sick, your mind can be sick as well? My husband said he did not know where the hospital was, but I boldly and adamantly spoke up and said, "I do!" My daughter said I asked her what she thought I should do. And she answered, "Mommy, it is up to you." (All the while, she made sure she highlighted the fact that it was Thanksgiving weekend, and most likely all offices would be closed. And even if they were open, they probably would not start any new intakes.)[19] I did not need any persuasion. I quickly said, "I want to go to Sheppard Pratt," and quickly put on my coat, signaling my immediacy.

The drive to Sheppard Pratt was tense. My husband continued to try to contact other providers to avoid my going to Sheppard Pratt, but he was unsuccessful. He definitely was averse to my decision to seek psychiatric help. My daughter told me I said, "Vannie please put that phone down

---

[19] Cianni said the insurance representative had instructed her on how to persuade me into choosing to go to Sheppard Pratt.

and just concentrate on driving!" I had made my choice, and that was the best news I had heard in a long time. I did not want anything or anybody to hinder me from going where I believed I would find help. I was anticipating relief. I wanted relief. Relief was in my sight and that was my top priority! Like it or not, Van would just have to deal with it. It was all about me! Finally, we arrived at the Sheppard Pratt campus, ironically located less than 10 minutes from where I live. Initially, we went to the wrong entrance, and my husband was irritating me. I wanted him to let my daughter out of the car so she could ask for directions to the Crisis Center, but he kept right on circling the same area. Perhaps he was stalling, trying to put off the inevitable.[20] I was weak, and I was desperate. I pleaded with my husband. "Vannie," I said, "please! You are not helping me here. Just let Skeet[21] out so she can ask someone where the Crisis Center is."

It was a bright, cheery, and sunny day in November (in stark contrast to my dark and forlorn spirit) when Cianni and I walked into the Sheppard Pratt facility. My husband stayed behind to park the car. Cianni and I followed the signs that led to the Crisis Center, and I nervously signed the log-in sheet. "How in the world did I ever get here? Mental illness? Really?" That was not supposed to be part of my story, but there I was at Sheppard Pratt writing another chapter in my life.

I took a seat and continued picking at my fingers, something I had been doing off and on the entire ride. My husband still had not come into the Crisis Center, so my daughter asked if I would be okay if she left me to go look for him. I sheepishly said I would, as I looked around at the other patients in the room. There was a family in the waiting area (husband, wife, and a young boy. The boy was being seen). Then there was a middle-aged man. Though I felt a sense of relief, I still felt out of place and hurt that I had to be there. Step. Step. Wobble. Wobble.

My husband and daughter returned. After two other persons were called, finally, the intake coordinator called my name. My husband rose from his seat to accompany me, but my daughter suggested I go alone. After all, I repeatedly said I wanted to talk to somebody. She thought if I wanted to talk to anybody in the family, I would have. She wanted me to be free to say whatever was on my mind to the mental health professionals.

---

[20] I think he was probably just as afraid as I was. What would become of his wife?
[21] My daughter's nickname.

I followed the intake coordinator slowly down the short hallway. We entered her small office. I was so afraid. My fear increased because I had to go alone. I knew Van and Cianni were only a short distance from me in the outer waiting area, but that was still too far away. Fear does not make sense.

What would this woman ask me? What if this was going to be just another door shut in my face? What if she found I did need help and I would have to be admitted for a week? Two weeks? Three weeks? What if? What if? What if? My mind was so confused. I knew I wanted and needed help. But at the same time, I might have been too afraid to accept the help I really needed. The intake coordinator was professional and handled me with care. She mentioned to me the possibility of entering into a program called, "The Adult Day Hospital." This program would allow me to be admitted as an outpatient. It was a two-week program and required I come to the hospital every weekday from 8:30 am to 3:30 pm.

After seeing the intake coordinator, I was taken to another room—very small with only a desk and a few chairs. I do not remember any pictures on the walls or anything that made this room appealing. It felt really clinical to me. Sitting at the desk was an attractive woman with a soothing smile and demeanor who further talked to me about what I was going through. I later learned she was the psychiatrist who would be assigned to my case. I had a brief conversation with Dr. Kaur, and then Van and Cianni were allowed to sit in the session with me. Cianni told me when she joined me in the office my countenance was better, suggesting I had been given a ray of hope. Why this brief moment of brightness? Was it because Dr. Kaur said she would help me? Was it because after our brief encounter she believed I was a good candidate for the Sheppard Pratt Adult Day Hospital Program? Or, did my face reflect the joy that comes from an answered prayer? Finally help was not just on the way, but it was here!

When Van and Cianni entered the room, they found me sitting in the far, right chair from the door, sunk down, rubbing my hands, and twiddling my thumbs nervously. Though Cianni caught a glimpse of my spirit lifted, my eyes were still weak and lifeless—no dancing, no sparkle—just a dull, clouded over, gloomy gaze. It is said "the eyes are the windows to the soul." I suppose anyone who looked into my eyes could see what a dreary, downtrodden, and cheerless soul I had become.

Dr. Kaur asked me questions about myself, and then she asked them questions about me.[22] I guess we answered her questions in a manner, whereby, she could do nothing else but agree. I needed to be seen immediately! It was the Thanksgiving holiday and nothing could be done for at least four days. If I got any worse, I suppose I could always call 911. *Sigh.* Dr. Kaur encouraged me that Thanksgiving was a time to be with family and people who loved and cared for me anyway. She reassured me I would be okay.

God is so very good. Even when you cannot seem to find Him, He is still there and caring for His children. Perhaps I felt alone and confused, and maybe doubtful that God was hearing my prayers; but on that day, God made it very obvious He had not left me alone.

The Adult Day Hospital Program can only receive a few patients at a time, and they were just about at their capacity; but God had a space for me. The intake coordinator told me there was an available space on the Tuesday after Thanksgiving. I could come into the Crisis Center on that Monday for what they called a "Bridge," which is an appointment to see a psychiatrist in order to assess me one final time before I enrolled into the program. Tuesday, November 27, 2012, I would finally start my therapy. I was scared but happy at the same time. Finally, I felt like I was on my way to becoming whole again.

The next day was Thanksgiving. My family and I always attend worship service before we enjoy our meal together. I always love Thanksgiving worship service. My home church, Saint Abraham Baptist, is lively. We sing songs of praise, thanksgiving, and adoration to God. Many stand up to give their personal testimonies of how God has blessed them through the year. The preacher delivers a powerful and enthusiastic sermon that brings people to their feet with joy and have them lifting their voices with shouts of praise. Some may even dance in the Spirit as they rejoice in God's word. I usually join in with the high praise, but this year it was so different. The fear and sadness would not release me to be joyous.

I walked gingerly through the double glass doors of my church (or did I shuffle as I had begun to do in fear I would fall again); down the short hallway; through another set of double glass doors, and into the

---

[22] As told to me by my daughter because I have no recollection of this

sanctuary, clinging tightly to my daughter for support. We took our seat. I cannot remember feeling anything but numb. As I reflect back on this time, I see myself as an expressionless paper doll or cardboard. No face, no voice, no depth. I believe it wasn't until my father began preaching one of his dynamic and passionate sermons from the Psalms that I came alive. I cannot remember the exact Psalm or the title of his sermon, but I do remember two words that gave me hope, "Preserved me." Suddenly, it became clear to me that despite all I was going through—the sadness, the panic, the fear, the loss of appetite, the nausea, and diarrhea, God had preserved me. I had not died. I was still alive! Alive to tell my story. Alive to share with family and friends. Alive! Alive! Alive!

Later that day, my husband and I joined my family at one of my sister's houses for dinner. I have a large, lively family. We love each other. We always laugh, talk, and act silly when we get together. Thanksgiving dinner was a great time, but not today. Much to my sadness, my daughter and I were separated. I went to the family dinner with my husband. I was surrounded by the people I love most in the world, but they all seemed like perfect strangers. I was too afraid of them to leave my husband's side. How could I be afraid of my own family? My mother and father are the sweetest people on the planet, and my siblings, nieces, and nephews are all a delight. But the phantom of fear had stolen the joy and peace I normally would have while in their presence. So, I spent the evening sitting in a corner of the room, cuddled up underneath the arm of my husband as if I had never seen these people a day in my life.

I am sure my family knew something was wrong with me. I decided it was now time for me to share my secret that I was going to be admitted into an outpatient program at a mental health facility. The confusion, the sadness, and the fear I was feeling were reflected in the eyes of my sisters as I broke the news to them. It was evident that for that brief moment in time, we were sharing the same feelings. Love is truly amazing. It will not allow you to suffer alone, but it will jump in the pain with you and share what you feel. Thanksgiving dinner came to an end, and my husband and I left to go home. It would be a long weekend for me.

I am a woman of faith, and the Bible is my guide to living. I can always find a biblical character to parallel my life story with. It is helpful to see people who walked through life and experienced the same struggles and to see how God came to their rescue every time. As I look back on my intake experience at Sheppard Pratt, I can see similarities in my story and that of King David's story reflected in the Psalms. He was a man acquainted with trouble; it was no stranger to him. He was also used to dealing with many enemies—King Saul (his father-in-law) and Absalom (his son) being among them. David knew what it was like to be surrounded by trouble; trouble that would cause him to fear for his very life. Yet, David was also acquainted with the God who would never leave him and who would preserve his life. Despite being surrounded by trouble, on every side, David could trust that His God would rescue him and deliver him. David's dilemma? He had to walk through the dark valley of trouble. God's response? "Preserve David's life."[23]

Like David, I was in trouble. Fear surrounded me. Everywhere I looked, there was fear. It never took a break. Morning, noon, and night fear pounced upon me as a lion pounces on his prey. My dilemma? I was in deep trouble. God's response? "Preserve my life." God did not let me die in the pit of despair. No. God sent me help in the form of the Sheppard Pratt Adult Day Hospital. Hallelujah!

---

[23] Psalm 138:7

Chapter Five

FACING MY OWN DEMONS

"My thoughts trouble me and I am distraught because of what my enemy is saying, because of the threats of the wicked; for they bring down suffering on me and assail me in their anger." Psalm 55:2b-3 (NIV)

Once I had the fall, I could not shake the thoughts that haunted me that I would fall again. Those were not the only thoughts that swirled in my mind like a strong wind blowing across freshly fallen snow. It was as if my mind had become like a snow globe. It was confined, imprisoned, and anything that shook me caused irrational thoughts to swirl about it.

Oh, how I wished the thoughts would stop racing through my head. Most of them were lies, and I knew it. Yet, I could not stop believing they might be true. Old lies like, "Your husband doesn't support you; your family doesn't support you; people don't love you; they aren't your friends; or you have no friends." With each lie, I guess I was sinking deeper and deeper into the pit of despair without really knowing it. It is amazing. After you hear lies for a period of time, they start to sound like the truth. Some of them were the same lies I had heard years before in 2003. Yes, I do remember the year because I was experiencing some of the same feelings now that I had felt then. I remember fear rose up against me like a lion lunging forward to devour its prey; even though now, the fear was more intense.

The day finally arrived when I would begin the journey to face my own demons—to face every lie and unravel the truth that was tucked deep inside. It would not be easy, but it was necessary. Finally, Tuesday,

November 27, 2012, arrived. I had been in the dark and fearful place for so long—too long. I could not help thinking if I would ever get better and if I was doing the right thing by going to Sheppard Pratt. But deep down inside, I knew if I was to ever get better, I needed to garner all the strength I could find and take it one step at a time. Step. Step. Wobble. Wobble. My thoughts and my emotions were all over the place, and I knew it was not true, but part of me felt like God had just forgotten all about me. I was so lost, so lonely, and felt so abandoned. Where was God when I needed Him the most?

The day was sunny and bright, but my spirit was dark and dismal as I cautiously and shyly left the warmth and safety of my husband's black Toyota Avalon. You know what's funny? I named the car Joshua; and right then, it was indeed my salvation, taking me to the place of true deliverance. I made my way through the automatic double doors, down the long unfamiliar hallway, rounded the corner to my left, and through the threshold that lead me to the Sheppard Pratt Adult Day Hospital. This was a world I was not familiar with, the world of those who struggled with mental illness.

The staff was pleasant and accommodating. They immediately began the process of admitting me into the program and instructing me of where to go and what to do. I cannot fully remember, but I believe my husband was there for a part of the process. Then, he was asked to leave. *("No Van. Don't leave me here with these strangers.")* Much to my surprise, all the patients looked "normal," including me. The way they were gathered around the counter where the snacks were and chatting together, they all just looked like coworkers getting their morning breakfast before moving off to their separate desks to begin another work day. I supposed it would not be long before some new person would come and think the same thing about me.

This was too much to take in. I thought to myself, "Oh no... I am here... But, I need to be here." Some parts of me were so glad to be there, but others parts said, I did not belong. I felt like a fish out of water. This should not be happening to me. But it was. From November 27, 2012, to December 11, 2012, (thank God it wasn't any longer) I made my way to Sheppard Pratt Hospital and spent each day looking at me! That was something I did not want to do. Oh, I could easily see the problems of others, but not mine.

The morning routine was always the same—check the board to see what nurse I was assigned to, go to her room, and fill out the form that asked the same questions every day, i.e., "How did you sleep? Did you feel like killing yourself last night? How many hours did you sleep? How is the medication working for you? What did you do last night? What are your goals for today?" Then, I had to see the nurse to discuss what I filled out on the form and to address any concerns or problems I was having. I then waited until it was time for the first group session.

Although it was sometimes difficult to go through this early morning process and sometimes I even thought, totally unnecessary, I came to realize it was very necessary and important for the professionals to get to the root of my issue. The only way to do that was to get me to look deep within myself and my life. I had to carefully examine my feelings, my thoughts, my life choices, and my surroundings. I had begun a journey to search for the truth, and God used these dedicated professionals to help me in that search. One thing was for sure, I could never be healed if I was unwilling to follow the path set before me.

Each day was different, but each day was the same. It seemed like all of us in the program were in need of getting over the hump of our irrational, painful, and confusing thoughts. We all appeared to be broken and needed to be fixed. Yes, some more than others, but we were all in the same boat in this same span of time. There were some repeaters and some newbies like myself. There were some who had spent days and/or weeks as inpatients, but now they were in transition, hoping to be free from the confinement of a mental hospital. But we all shared a common thread and that was a mind that was sick in some way. There we were with either a diagnosis of bipolar disorder, depression, anxiety disorder, panic disorder, obsessive compulsive disorder, or drug and alcohol addiction, or a combination. You name it. It was in that room. Most of us were strangers. Although, there were some who had crossed paths before and knew each other and were familiar with the professional staff.

For the most part, we looked "normal" on the outside, meaning if we had been found in another situation, we would not have guessed that most of us had mental illnesses. We did not walk around like zombies.

We knew what day and year it was. Our bodies were clean and our clothing appropriate. We were still doing life as best we could—some still taking care of their families, working, driving, etc., although maybe with limitations. The point is, we were not "babbling idiots" who had no concept of time or space. We were a group of functioning individuals who somehow lost our way in the jungle of life and became entangled in the vines of dysfunction and disorder. Something triggered our disorders that might have been lying dormant for years, months, weeks, or days and brought it to the surface so that now the mundane things of life had somehow become impossible to handle. Life had taken a dive and we had spiraled out of control. Now here we were, thankfully, in the safety net of the Sheppard Pratt Adult Day Program. Thank God.

Day-after-day, the professionals at the hospital worked with us and cared for us. They always treated us with respect and were patient with us. Dr. Kaur followed me while I was in the program. She diagnosed me with anxiety and major depression. Much to my sadness, I was prescribed medication. After a brief period of getting used to the medications, which caused morning nausea and diarrhea, the meds proved to be beneficial. They helped me sleep and balanced out my mood.

During my time at Shepperd Pratt, I found the mental health field to be amazing and quite interesting. We spent our days in support groups talking about our lives and learning how to take back the control we had lost. We were taught new skills to promote right thinking, such as Cognitive Behavioral Therapy (also known as CBT). Art and music were also used as ways to promote healing, along with medication and talk therapy.

The common thread of mental illness made it easier for me to connect with many of the patients in the program, and these people helped me to get through each day. I found myself thinking of my new "friends" often and praying for them, hoping that soon life would be better for them too.

A healing team of professionals and patients were formed, and together we forged our way to better mental health. As a result, one-by-one, patients were released from the program. I was one of them. What was strange was I was fearful of coming to Sheppard Pratt, but now as I faced being released, I experienced a new fear. Sheppard Pratt had held my hand and helped me through the most horrible time of my life. I had become comfortable with the program, the surroundings, and the patients. I was not sure if I would be able to make it on my own. I had learned how to "do life" while in the program, but would I be able to handle my life without this special and much needed help? I really had nothing to fear because before I was released, I was given the name of a psychiatrist and names of therapists to choose from for my aftercare.

Recovery would be a process, but I was willing to do what needed to be done in order to be whole. I entered the road with many troubling thoughts and great anguish. But the closer I got to the end, the less troubling those thoughts were. I learned strategies and received information that continues to help me even today when I find depression, anxiety, and or panic trying to overwhelm me. I thank God so much for Sheppard Pratt Mental Hospital. It was such a blessing to me. Because of the dedicated professionals and staff of the Adult Day Hospital, I did not drown in the darkness that had threatened to take my life.

It is amazing how much power our thoughts have over our lives. I was overwhelmed by irrational and troubling thoughts I knew came from the kingdom of darkness but was hard to dismiss and hard to change to new and positive ones. I guess I felt like the biblical psalmist in Psalm 55 who said his thoughts were a source of distress and anguish for him. What do you do when the enemy is in you? What do you do when you take everything that causes you angst with you everywhere you go? All you can do is cry, press forward, and trust that God will help you and hold you together.

Chapter Six

ANGELS IN SKIN FACES

"Finally, all of you, be like-minded, be sympathetic, love one another, be compassionate and humble" 1 Peter 3:8 (NASB)

What a blessing it is to have people to walk with you through the dark valley of depression and anxiety. God was gracious to me. He surrounded me with family, friends, coworkers, and members of the body of Christ to support me with their prayers and acts of kindness. These were people who were in pain, suffering in silence, and just as confused as I was but still did whatever they could to help me in my time of distress. I was never alone. One such person was my coworker, Kim. She has always been such a blessing to me. This time was no different. When I asked her if she had begun to see a difference in my behavior prior to my breakdown, what she described to me was beautiful, enlightening, and yet sad. She took me back to the summer months of 2012. I had no idea any of this was going on with me. I thought I was fine, but not so. She helped me to see me. I am going to let Kim speak in her own words what she noticed about me.

> "I started to notice changes in Pam around May of 2012, just prior to her going to her yearly ministry retreat in Virginia. I had noticed prior to the retreat, Pam was looking tired, was a little forgetful, and not as organized at times. She looked as if she needed to be energized, as if she needed a nice, long, relaxing vacation. I thought the retreat would be the fix. But sadly, when Pam returned

from her retreat, she was not her vibrant self. She was not
full of energy, and she was not rested. The retreat did not
fix Pam, which I thought was very odd. She always came
back from the yearly retreats a little tired, but yet rested—
full of new, bright ideas of how to worship and share the
Lord with others. She would always tell me about the new
"hook-ups" she made, the new acquaintances she met,
the new preaching robe she bought for a bargain, and the
new projects she thought of for her ministry "Wind of
Change"; but not this time. She came back worse and it
was very noticeable. I was not sure why, and for a while,
I thought it was just me. I thought maybe I did not give
Pam a chance to tell me about her new journey—stories
of her retreat.

As time went on, I started to notice that my dear friend,
the sister I wish I had, was getting worse. But I just did
not know what it was. She did not smile anymore, laugh
anymore, or go out to lunch with her friends anymore. She
even didn't seem happy about the ministry anymore. She
didn't seem happy about much of anything anymore, even
family and God. These two subjects, family and God, my
friend did not talk about too much anymore, which was
really odd and a bit scary.

I remember trying to engage Pam in a conversation
after one holiday. She had a hard time telling me about
anything that had happened at her parents' house, which
was another sign to me that something was really wrong.
On this particular occasion, everyone in Pam's family was
going to be at this big cookout. I remember that Thursday
leading up to the family get-together, I had mentioned to
Pam how nice her family event was going to be and how
I could not wait to hear all the details on Monday. Pam's
response was a blank, tired stare. All Pam said in a flat,

emotionless tone was, "Yeah I forgot about that," and just walked on by.

I remember telling my mom about my concerns for Pam. My mom said she could be depressed, or maybe there could be something medically wrong. My mother told me to keep an eye on her and pray. By late summer, things had gotten much worse. I think by mid-August or September, I knew Pam was depressed. I did not know what to do. I did not know the extent of her depression. Not only was my friend fighting this deep depression; she had another battle going on that I was not aware of until much later. It was a spiritual battle, which is far worse, far scarier, and much harder to dig yourself out of. The only way I can describe Pam during the fall of 2012, is that she had lost who she was. She lost her soul (mind, will and emotions), her spirit, and her way. She was falling, and it seemed like nothing could be done. She was not thinking clearly, nor functioning fully. Her work was suffering. She looked permanently lost. But it was not just me who noticed. Others at work had come to me with their concerns about Pam. I would just tell them she was tired, or she was just a little under the weather. I did not want to lie to them, nor did I want to tell them what was really wrong or what I had suspected. I was afraid to let them know.

There are several examples of what I noticed concerning Pam. But, I will only mention the two that struck me the most during the Fall of 2012. The first one (which Pam and I now laugh about from time-to-time) was "Hurricane Pam." I guess looking back, this name is befitting in an odd sense as this was truly what Pam was going through—her personal hurricane. The state we live in hardly ever gets hurricanes. But during this particular October, our state issued a hurricane warning. Maryland issued warnings for everyone to stay off of the roads and to stay at home. The institute where Pam and I worked issued a liberal leave policy the day before. Well guess who did not stay home, Pam. She actually drove into work and walked from the parking garage to our building with the help of a fellow friend. Pam only stayed for a little while before realizing she needed to go home. This is just an example of the confusion Pam was going through.

The second event was when Pam's son-in-law brought her by the office for a few minutes to visit. I went down to the lobby. When I saw the car pull up, I decided to go outside to meet her. I remember starring at Pam as she was trying to walk up the street. She was walking up to the building, but she was clinging to the wall while walking. You could tell, she was very weak and frail. She could barely stand and she was crying. We never made it to the office; we just sat in the lobby and talked. Eventually, I walked her back to the car where her son-in-law was waiting. We were walking so… slow. She was holding onto my arm really tight, pressing against the side of me like she was afraid she would fall or would not make it to the car. This was the last time I saw Pam, until she came back from her leave of absence.

I am not sure why this happened to Pam, why she had to go through this. But I think every battle you go through, you come out much stronger, and you take your lessons you have learned and pass them on to help others, if possible. For Pam, in my opinion, I think part of that lesson was learning to take care of herself, to learn to ask for help when she needed it, and to learn just how strong a person she really was and is. For years, Pam was always running around doing this and doing that. And although the tasks she was doing were things she loved, she never stopped to take a break or rest. She just kept going, just like the energizer bunny. But eventually everyone burns out, whether physically, emotionally, and/or spiritually, if they do not take care of themselves. Sometimes you have to fall down to learn and wake up and realize *you* need attention and love. I do not think Pam was doing that for herself. She was always too busy helping others. She should have been helping and loving herself too.

I have mixed emotions in what I am about to say, and what I am about to say might sound odd or mean. It is not my intent. I am sorry this happened to my dear friend, and I wish it had not happened; but looking back, I think this had to happen. Pam came out of this a much stronger and confident person. I know for a fact, her hardships during this time period (both emotionally and spiritually) have helped other people. I believe Pam is able to reach out to others because of this experience and truly help them. She helps people to feel they are not alone, that mental illness can happen to anyone, and they can get through it. God gives everyone gifts. But unfortunately, 90% of us (in my opinion) do not realize our gifts. God's gift to Pam is her heart, her care for others, and how she shares herself with everyone. I believe God wanted Pam to realize and finally see what she was worth, and how she needed to be taken care of as well."

Many of my friends had committed themselves to fasting and praying for me. They were faithful. I could count on them like clockwork. Whenever I think of this, I can't help but remember Maxine. Maxine is a dear, sweet sister in Christ and a fervent prayer warrior. If you ask Maxine to pray for you, you can count on God hearing her prayer. When I told Maxine I was in need of prayer, she immediately promised she would fast and pray. And pray she did! For many mornings around the same time (about 5:00 am, which happened to be the time I seemed always to awake in panic), Maxine would send a powerful text prayer. Lying awake full of anxiety in the darkness, I remember hearing the familiar ding of my cell phone signaling help was there with me. I may have been by myself in the room, but I was not alone. Maxine faithfully showed up every morning and her fired up, passionate prayers, warmed my heart and encouraged me that someone was thinking of me. I cannot say I always welcomed the prayers because sometimes the spiritual warfare going on inside of me would not allow me to accept what God was doing through Maxine's prayers, but those times were few. More often than not, I appreciated Maxine so very much. Her prayers were a source of strength and hope, and I looked forward to them.

There were others of my friends who could empathize with me because they themselves had already been through some of the same things or were currently battling their own tormenting demons. They put their own feelings and fears aside so they could join me in the battle or sit with me in the place of despair to offer me encouragement.

Yes, God sent angels in skin faces, people who faithfully heard and heeded His voice to come see about me. They showed up at the time in my life when I needed them most and offered me their homes, their beds to sleep in, their food to eat, their time, and their attention. It was all wrapped up beautifully in their love for me. Their actions spoke louder than any words ever could as they followed God's command to be loving, sympathetic, and compassionate. I became their top priority. They would put their lives on hold, so they could come to my rescue.

Even now, I can see their faces stained with tears, as they watched me go through. I can see their faces perplexed and confused by what they saw. I can see their faces, somber, drawn, and fearful. But more than that, I can see their hearts full of faith and hope that soon God would bring their wife, mother, grandmother, daughter, sister, friend, and coworker back from wherever she was to the comforting world of family and friends.

Chapter Seven

PRAYING MY WAY
THROUGH THE STORM

"When the righteous cry for help, the Lord hears and delivers
them out of all their troubles." Psalm 34:17 (ESV)

You know, I did not think I was praying through those dark weeks of trouble, but my prayer journal says otherwise. Throughout those weeks of uncertainty, fear, depression, anxiety, and numbness, my spirit was still crying out to the only One Who could help me. I was driven by my pain and fear into the arms of the One Who promised to be a shelter for me. These are some of my prayers (straight from my journal) to Abba, my Heavenly Father, and I know He heard and answered every one.

October 19, 2012

Dear Abba,

Thank You for getting me through that. Please heal me and make me whole. I don't know what happened or why, but I know You do. Please continue to be with me and help me not to fear. You are here, and You will help me. Hallelujah! You are "I Am!"…Thank you Lord! You've got me.

Another thing that episode showed me is that I am not in control, and things can happen very quickly. I didn't have time to think, and I didn't have time to pray. Before I knew it, I was down. Father, death will come just like that. I may not have time to think about getting right. Please help me to live my life so that no matter what happens, I will be at peace with You!

Please help me not to be fearful. In Jesus' name. Amen.

October 20, 2012

Dear Abba,

Thank You for blessing me to live to see another day. Thank You that I'm up and didn't have a falling episode. I'm cold and a little weak but other than that, I feel better than I did yesterday. My hands are shaky, so it's hard for me to write.

Yesterday, I spent the whole day in bed. I was queasy all day. Skeet came over after work and she sat with me until midnight. She fed me, gave me drinks, and gave me medicine to help me sleep. What a blessing she is! Thank You for her.

Although I feel better than yesterday, I am still weak and cold. My hands were white and my lips a little pale when I woke up. I want to climb back into bed, but I can't. *(I had a workshop to teach on that day.)*

Oh Lord, I need Your help! Something is wrong and I need Your help. P.S. My leg still hurts from where the cramp was. Maybe this was no ordinary cramp.

October 22, 2012

Dear Abba,

Thank You so much for this brand, new day. I was so afraid but You were with me.

Even now I am afraid. My legs are shaking like it is cold, but I know it's not. I know I am afraid to go to the doctors, but I know I must go. I am tempted not to make the appointment, but I will because even though I am afraid that the doctor may say something I don't want to or are afraid of hearing, I want to know the truth so that I will be free. Jesus said I shall know the truth and the truth will make me free.

Yesterday was a good day overall. I felt less fearful than I had been for the past couple of days. I was home alone for about an hour or so between the time Van left for church and Skeet came over. She sticks right in there with me. No matter what! She fed me; changed my sheets; washed, folded, and put away all the laundry, and ministered to me when I was fearful. Everything almost seemed normal until it started getting dark and I knew Skeet had to leave. Van was home, then; but I don't feel as "safe and secure" with him. I feel "safe" with Skeet. Just when she was about to leave, I had a real wave of fear and needed someone to hold me. She came right in the room and laid over me, holding me close. I cried in her arms and asked her to pray for me and she did.

Abba, how can I thank You for my daughter? I can't thank You enough. She is definitely one of Your special blessings, Your grace that I don't deserve. Praise Your holy name!

October 24, 2012

Dear Abba,

You are my only help!!

The devil is a liar and a deceiver!! He is tempting me that I will fall out again. He is tempting me to give up trying to do anything. He says I can't finish school, I will have no strength to preach or teach, and I can't go back to work.

Abba, the devil is after my mind.

But, he can't have it because my mind belongs to You, Jesus!

Lord, I don't know right now whether You have sent this evil spirit or allowed it (II Corinthians 12:7). But I do know, You, oh God, controls it. When You decide enough is enough, it will flee NEVER to rise again.

Holy Spirit, rise up in me and give me POWER!!!

Abba, please keep me on my feet! I keep feeling like I will fall out. I feel worse today than I did yesterday.

October 25, 2012

Dear Abba,

You are the source of my strength! You are my Savior! The One who rescues me! Lord, You are strong! You are a Mighty Warrior! You are a safe Haven! When I am afraid, I will trust in You (Psalm 56:3).

God, You are angry because of the torment the devil is taking me through (Psalm 18:7). You are fighting on my behalf. Hallelujah! Glory!

Abba, thank You for Your great love! Thank You for deliverance! Thank You for just being You!

GLORY TO GOD!

October 26, 2012

Dear Abba,

I see Your mighty hand at work. You are so faithful! You have been holding me up, holding me together, and holding me close to You. Thank You. I could not have made it this far without You.

It's been such a struggle, Abba. Fear and dread have stalked me all week. BUT grace and mercy have overcome their attempts to destroy me. Hallelujah!!

Thank You for blessing me to complete my (ministry) assignments.

Thank You, Lord. This time last week I was just entering this battle. Today, I am closer to being through it than I was last week. Hallelujah! I press by Your Spirit to my victory! Glory!

I put myself in Your hands. Abba, take me one step at a time. In Jesus' name. Amen.

Oh, how I love You. Oh, how I want You. Oh, how I need You.

October 27, 2012

Dear Abba,

Thank You for another new and blessed day!

I was hoping I would have peace and would be able to sleep well here at Mommy and Daddy's house. But "It", the fear, has followed me. I woke up again around 4:00 or 4:30 or so in the morning, and I could feel the fear. My stomach was churning and I was very cold to the point of shaking. I tried praying and listening to the book of Matthew, but "It" didn't go away. (This fear is worse than some Halloween haunted house. This fear is deep in me.)

As I lay trembling, I must have drifted off a little because all of a sudden, I was sitting up in bed and that feeling I felt just before I fell out last Friday came over me. I could feel myself falling out. I tried screaming for Mommy but nothing came out. I couldn't even open my mouth. Then I woke up! Thank You Jesus; it was only a dream.

My stomach is still in knots. I went to the bathroom (I felt stable) and had a bowel movement. I looked in the mirror and I looked fine (no paleness).

I want peace and rest but it seems both have fled from me. Lord, please have mercy!

I cannot continue on this way. I know You can change the situation in a manner of seconds. Why haven't You, Abba?

Is there something I should be doing that I am not? Is there something I am not doing that I should be?

Why this horrible, horrible fear? O Lord, I need You!

You blessed me yesterday to finish the women's retreat. I enjoy seeing those ladies and look forward to being with them each year. Thank You for their love!

After we left the facility, Skeet and I stopped at Cracker Barrel to get breakfast. I could feel myself growing weak and once having to grab for Skeet. I went to the bathroom, but felt I was walking on egg shells. I ate a scrambled egg, some sausages, and half a piece of toast with jelly.

We left Cracker Barrel and went to Columbia Mall to get our eyebrows done. I look so much better. Hahaha.

While in the Mall, we went to the movies to see Alex Cross and played a video game. (I haven't done that in a long time). I think I felt more "normal" than I had in a week.

I am getting sleepy. Will You give me peace and rest in the Lord?

I was sleepy, but no sleep, no peace—only fear. Abba, I don't know what to do.

I am really sleepy again. But when I fall asleep, I wake back up in fear and can't sleep.

The devil is a liar!!

The light has come. Thank You for the light!

I'm staying at Mommy and Daddy's house for a few days because I can't stay at home and I don't want to be around Van right now.

When we went to pack my things yesterday, just being in the house and being around Van had me so unstable. I felt like I would pass out. But You held me, Lord. Thank You.

Of course, he didn't want me to go. And if Skeet wasn't there, he would have pounced all over me, telling me to stay.

At any rate, I am safe at my parents' house now. Please, Lord, help me be made whole here. I can't stay here forever. I've got a home, and I want to go home at some time.

The big house overhaul is Friday—cleaning, throwing out the old and bringing in the new! Hallelujah! Please help me think on the new.

I am going to class today. Please help me. In Jesus' name.

I am leaning on You, Lord. I am so very weak. I can't take one step or breathe one breath without You.

I love You and I know You love me.

Maybe today is the day for a complete breakthrough!

October 28, 2012

Dear Abba,

Wow! What a difference a day makes.

You blessed me yesterday to go to school. I was so happy to be there. I love my classes. Please give me strength to write my papers and do my presentation.

Today, Lord, You stood up in me and allowed me to preach with power. Thank You. That's where I need to be—in ministry full-time. I need to get out of the workplace. Please, Lord, help me.

Father, I pray never to have any falling out experiences again. Please bless my physical health. Help me not to be stressed and afraid. I trust You for total victory!

Please help Van!

Our hearts have been broken God! Please put us back together again. We really need a miracle.

I love You!

October 31, 2012

Dear Abba,

Thank You for blessing me to live to see another day. God, You are so very kind. I cannot make it each day without You!

Thank You when I got up, I felt strong and stable. Praise Your holy name.

I'm at Cianni and TC's house now. Yesterday was a really, really, rough day for me. My neck and shoulder were killing me, my head felt tight, and full of "something." I could not stand or move without feeling like I was about to fall over. I was so very fearful and nervous.

Mommy and Daddy were going to the Dollar Store and I was going with them, but it got so bad that Mommy said she would stay home with me while Daddy ran errands. Before leaving, Daddy and Mommy prayed for me, and Mommy also laid her hands all over my body (beginning with my legs). Mommy and I had a good talk about a lot of things—perfectionism, control, other sin issues, and menopause. In fact, Mommy thinks I'm dealing with menopausal issues (she said one of my sisters has been going through the same types of things). I had texted Cianni to say I was really going through and she came by. Thank You for Cianni.

Breakfast was delicious and I really ate well. Cianni helped me gather my things and she brought me here to her house.

On the way, we stopped at the Post Office and my house. Van wasn't there. I'm so glad. We picked up a heavier coat for me and a couple of sweaters, etc. It has gotten colder since the hurricane (Sandy) blew through.

Everything was pretty much shutdown yesterday— banks, post offices, schools, some government agencies, and my workplace.

One of my sisters texted us this morning to say she was taking Daddy to the hospital. I am so glad I wasn't there. I would have been such a hindrance, and I don't know how I would handle sitting in the ER for an undetermined amount of time.

I talked to Van last night. He wants me to come back home, but I'm not ready yet. I don't think I can handle being there by myself with Van yet. And I don't think he can handle what I'm going through yet, either.

God, what am I going through? I feel stuck. I feel like there's no way out!

I did call the counselor's office. They were closed, too. I hope they call back today so I can get an appointment.

Cianni's house has come alive. Cianni has already left for work. TC is up and I just heard him wake my grandson up.

Thank You Lord for life. Please help me live mine to the fullest today! In Jesus' name. Amen.

I still love You!

December 30, 2012

Dear Abba,

You bring me joy! You are my hope! All that I need can be found in You! Praise Your holy name!

Daddy, You gave me such a good day yesterday. I felt like me! Thank You!

I started the day off by going to my therapist. It was her first day and my first day, too. I really like her. She's calming. She's knowledgeable. She appears understanding and non-judgmental. We spent about 45 minutes together, and I unloaded and cried; but it felt so good. I felt so free after talking to her. I can't wait until our next session. Hahaha. Thank You, Father, for Your provision. You know exactly what I need, and You are meeting that need. Hallelujah! Please bless this counselor abundantly and give her wisdom and discernment concerning me. In Jesus' name. Amen.

The rest of the day was spent playing with Cianni. Thank You for her. She brings me so much joy! We laughed, we joked, we handled business—my personal business and my ministry business. This was especially good for me because I hadn't been able to do much for the ministry. Thank You, Jesus! You are wonderful! (I know life isn't a party and I know things are different when you actually live with people, but I wish Cianni lived with us. That's really selfish and unrealistic. Isn't it? Yes, it is.) Cianni and I even went shopping. We had fun putting together my telescope (she really did it. I just held the box so she could see the picture. Hahaha). Oh, what fun I had yesterday, all day. Thank You so very much, Jesus!

Daddy, I didn't have one anxiety attack yesterday. Thank You a gazillion times! I got a cramp in my left leg this morning, but this time it wasn't an issue. Thank You Jesus!

Extend Your grace and Your mercy. In Jesus' name. Amen.

January 1, 2013

Dear Abba,

Hallelujah! You've blessed my family, friends, and me to live to see another year. Thank You. You are kind to us.

Father, only You know the path my life should take, will take. Please, Holy Spirit breathe on me, and guide me and lead me through each day. I need Your wisdom, Your power, Your strength.

Lord, You are my Rock, my Strong Tower, and my Fortress. I seek Your face. I long for You. I am thirsty for You. I crave Your Presence.

Please renew me, revive me, resurrect me, and restore me.

Father, thank You for my testimony. It is being a blessing to so many men and women alike. Last night, with tears in his eyes, one of the men of the church thanked me for sharing, and then one of the deacons thanked me and called me a "soldier." Wow! Father, You are turning my pain into a source of praise. Be glorified in all of it. I trust You to provide everything I need! You are my portion; therefore, I will trust You.

Thank You, Jesus! You've brought me a mighty long way in such a short period of time. Hallelujah! God, You are so very good to me! I can't thank You enough! Amen.

January 5, 2013

Dear Abba,

Thank You so much for blessing my family and me to see another day. You are so very merciful. Thank You that I have not had an anxiety attack this morning, and I feel better today than I did yesterday morning.

Yesterday morning I woke up feeling a little bit nauseous. After going to the bathroom and being up a little bit, I started having an attack. It started in my stomach. It felt like it was on fire, and then it spread so that my entire body inside started feeling like it was on fire. I got real nervous and felt afraid to leave the bed. I didn't wake Van because I knew he'd only say, "You know what to do." I can't stand when he says that. I'm seeking help and support, and he just leaves me out there. I texted Cianni to let her know what was happening. (She always wants to know when I have an episode.) She asked if I wanted her to come. I said, "Yes." I was feeling really nervous, and I knew Van had to leave for work. I didn't want to be here by myself. Thank You, Abba, that Cianni came right over. By the time she got here, the nervousness was starting to subside and the burning had ceased. I was left feeling a little jittery, but I was able to at least get out of the bed. I didn't want to spend my day there. Thank You, Lord, for handling another attack and rendering it powerless to harm me. Thank You that when I get those real crazy attacks, You've blessed me to be at home and near my bed. You take care of me. Thank You.

When Cianni came, we sat on the couch for a while. I shared some of my journal and illustrations with her. She told me she had expected me to have an attack because she's noticed that I am taking on (mentally and emotionally) too much and it's leading me backwards. She helped me identify some things I needed to release so I can concentrate on taking care of me, i.e., let Van get up on his own (when I'm not here he does it. It's his responsibility to get himself up and out to handle his business—I do!); let Van take care of his own health (he's fine. He can make his own appointments, etc.); be assertive—speak up when I need to say what I need; don't overwork at work; don't internalize; don't turn things into a catastrophe. Father, You blessed me the rest of the day, and I enjoyed it. Thank You.

Abba, You lifted me. You strengthened me, gave me courage, and helped me forget the anxiety of my morning. Thank You. Your grace won't leave me in a bad place. Hallelujah!

Today I see my therapist. I can't wait. Please bless our session. Have Your perfect way. Thank You for providing the money and insurance. Glory to Your name. Amen.

January 6, 2013

Dear Abba,

You are the love of my life! Nothing and nobody compares to You. You alone are God. El Shaddai, all I need is found in You. Let me drink deeply from Your fountain of supply. In You, Jehovah, I find hope, help, health, and happiness. In You, Yahweh, I find love, life, and laughter. In You, Jesus, I find salvation, security, safety, and supply. In You, Holy Spirit, I find sanctification, joy, comfort, and peace. I need You God. Everything I need and want is in You.

Father, thank You. Yesterday, I did not have any strange attacks. Please keep fear, panic and anxiety, and depression far away from me. Bind them, oh Lord, and release courage, joy, merriment, and trust in You. Let me never lose sight of You—even if I can't see You. Let my spirit always connect with You.

My life is out of balance. I have spent so much time working that I don't know how to play. I am also finding out that I have friends and family who love me dearly, but I don't have "playmates." Father, I don't know how to find them, but I know You know exactly who and what I need. Will You send me some girlfriends designed just for me, somebody who will play with me, someone who will strengthen me, and someone I can strengthen? Daddy, You supply all my needs!

Thank You for my counselor. Bless her, save her, love her.

Give me health, Lord.

I love You. Amen.

January 7, 2013

Dear Abba,

You are phenomenal! Thank You for being a restorer. Piece by piece You are putting my life back together.

My psychiatrist appointment is tomorrow. Please bless Dr. Singh and give us a great patient-doctor relationship. I trust You in all of this, Abba.

Yesterday, when I came home from church, I was starting to feel a little jittery because I wasn't real happy about coming home. But I talked to Van about some things that were on my heart, and the jitters ceased. Thank You. Please help me be assertive, and teach me how to communicate my feelings.

January 9, 2013

Dear Abba,

Thank You for getting me through the night. I was so fearful about taking 20 mg of Celexa instead of 10 mg.

But You blessed me, and I did not have an adverse reaction like I did with Zoloft.

Lift me back up. I went to see Dr. Singh yesterday. I was nervous and panicky all day. We didn't talk long but he said 10 mg of Celexa was a child's dose and he wanted to up it to 20 mg. He also said he wanted to wean me off the Klonipin because it's addictive. Please Lord, let me get off that medicine. I don't want to be addicted to anything but Your… love, mercy and grace. I think by changing the dosage of Celexa, he'll be able to wean me off. I was so afraid because I didn't know what to expect, but nothing happened (except what I may have concocted in my mind. Please Lord, renew my mind. It definitely needs to be changed). I like Dr. Singh. I am trusting You are leading and guiding me. I'll go if You go with me. Have mercy Father. I want to be made whole. Help me to know the truth so that I can be free. In Jesus' name. Amen.

January 14, 2013

Dear Abba,

I feel like I'm sinking. I feel like I'm going backwards. I feel like I won't get better. But none of that can be true. I need You so much, Lord.

I am so broken. The tears have returned. I am fighting and struggling against the winds and waves of hopelessness and loneliness.

I know the devil is a liar. Holy Spirit, come to my rescue. Rise up in me and give me power, strength, and courage to stand and fight.

Daddy, am I trusting You enough? Have I surrendered all? Have I moved out of the way? Am I still trying to control things? Daddy, I don't know.

One minute I feel like just giving up and the next minute I say I want to go on. Abba, I need You! Tell me where to go, what to think, what to do. I don't know what to do! I can't do this without You, Father. Please help me.

Abba, besides not feeling well emotionally and sometimes not feeling well physically, this is getting expensive—copays, doctors and hospital visits, medicine, and therapists. My money has taken wings and is flying away to the medical and psychiatric community.

Forgive me if I am complaining. I don't mean to be. I just need to tell You, Abba, how I feel and what is going on with me. You are the only One Who can help me.

Despite all I'm going through, I still love You.

Abba, what is the purpose of this test? What is Your promise to me? I will continue to wait. I will persevere, as long as You'll go with me. I can't do this by myself. Help me see You in this day. Carry me through. I am very weak. Your grace is sufficient!

January 15, 2013

Dear Abba,

I saw Dr. Singh yesterday, and we are starting the weaning from Klonopin. I am trusting You to do this Daddy. Please get me off this medicine, and don't let me ever have to go on it again. Dr. Singh suggested I see a therapist within their group so the two of them can collaborate concerning me. I thought that was a wise thing to do; so, I withdrew from the Brick Therapy Group and made an appointment with Carol Dunn.

January 20, 2013

Dear Abba,

It's hard to walk by faith when your mind is filled with lies. Please help me know the truth. Please forgive me if I am not doing this right. I need Your help. Forgive me if I'm ungrateful. Sometimes I'm confused and I know that comes from the devil. Jesus, teach me the truth.

January 26, 2013

Dear Abba,

My therapy session went well. I like Carol's techniques better than Sheila's. I think Carol is more who I need. We talked about my job situation, my desire to do ministry full-time, and my need for money and benefits. We talked about developing friendships. She said, I am more of the norm that I don't have close relationships from my school days. Carol is helping me see the truth. Thank You Lord. I have believed lies for so long, but You are helping me to know and see the truth that has always been there.

January 26, 2013

Dear Abba,

I am traveling through dangerous and unfamiliar territory. I am being hunted like prey. Provide a way of escape. Teach me how to war in the Spirit. Give me power Holy Spirit. I cannot do this alone. I am weak and fragile and afraid. I need You so I won't give up and give in.

Chapter Eight

GOD'S GRACE

"Each time He said, 'My grace is all you need.'"
2 Corinthians 12:9a (NLT)

"God is good all the time and all the time God is good." I could hear these words resounding throughout churches I had attended. I saw the people responding with fervor and gladness. But did I dare believe such a thing while I was in the deep, dark, pit of fear and depression? Was it possible that in the darkest place I had ever been in my life, the Light of the world was still present with me? Was it a false hope or could I actually believe that in the stench of rotten hopes, decaying dreams, and declining life, the One Who is called the Rose of Sharon and the Lily of the Valley would be there with me? And if He was there, where was He? Where was He in the blackness of the morning when I was brutally attacked by something I couldn't even see? Where was He when the spirit of fear draped itself over me like a tight-fitting garment? Where was He when I was about to drown in my own tears because of depression? Where was He?

I could not see Him then. Perhaps my eyes were too clouded by my tears. I could not see Him then. Maybe it was my inability to concentrate. But now as I look back on those days, I can see Him quite clearly. I can see Him in every footstep I made through the valley of the shadow of death. I can see Him carrying me and upholding me to keep me from falling again. I can hear His sweet voice encouraging me to just keep moving forward through the darkness, through the stench—just keep moving forward. I can see His Light guiding my way, His peace keeping me from totally losing it, His protection guarding me from the hosts of hell who wanted to destroy me, and His love embracing me and wiping away my tears.

Oh no, I could not see Him then, but I can see Him now. He was there all the time! He was leading me, helping me, watching me, protecting me, and providing for me. His grace was a shelter for me! God's grace sustained me, strengthened me, comforted me, lifted me, and loved me back to LIFE. Everything the devil stole, God restored and made it better. He made me better! God's overwhelming, astonishing, unstoppable, unspeakable, love overshadowed me. It overtook the plan of the devil to destroy me, overlooked all my faults and failures, and restored me. It overpowered decades of wrong thinking, wrong behaviors, and wrong beliefs. It renewed me, revived me, and resurrected me to life. Truly, old things have been destroyed, and new things have been erected (2 Corinthians 5:17).

It was God's grace that stood up in me every day and propelled me forward to go to Sheppard Pratt. I had no strength of my own. I was so fearful and weak, and I battled within myself to hold back screams or streams of tears. I remember one day in particular, I struggled (as I did every morning) through the nausea and diarrhea because of the medications taken the night before. I struggled through the fear associated with bathing myself, and I struggled through tears of sadness of losing my life as I once knew it and having to spend another day at a mental hospital. I did not want to go. God why? God knew how weak I was, and He knew I could not face another day at Sheppard Pratt; but He helped me. I was finally dressed and on my way. I remember standing in the kitchen with tears in my eyes and having a sinking feeling in my heart as I watched my husband walk out to the car to start it up and get it warm for me. I took my morning dosage of Klonopin for the anxiety, and I slowly moved toward the back door; but that was as far as I had the strength to go. It was as if I had come upon an invisible shield. My mind was crying out, "Please don't make me go." But in my spirit, I knew I had to go if I wanted to get better. I stood in the kitchen doorway that led to my backyard, but my feet would not move. I had lost the power, motivation, and strength to move forward. But the Lord sent my husband back to coax me, and the Lord gently nudged me forward. It was as if God put His loving hand on the small of my back and lightly pushed me out the door. If He had not done that, I do not know how long I would have just stood in the doorway.

God knew how much I really needed Him that day because I did not want to be at Sheppard Pratt. He knew that day would be an especially hard day for me. He knew I would cry in front of everyone—all those strangers—in my first support group session. He nudged me out the door anyway. Why? Because He knew the only way I could be free of the bondage of fear and depression that had become a part of my daily life was to go to the place of healing He had prepared just for me. He wanted to show me I could trust Him to keep all of His promises to me, especially the promise that He would not leave me or forsake me.[24] He wanted to teach me that His grace is all I need. He wanted me to be able to look back at one of the hardest days of my life and see Him working behind the scenes. I could not see Him then, but I can see Him clearly now. He was there through it all, and I only made it through that day because of His grace. Seeing Him then helps me to see Him now. Sheppard Pratt is not the hardest thing I will come upon in life. Life is difficult. Life is challenging. Life can be brutal. But God's grace can help me sail through every storm of life. God's grace can help me persevere through the fog of fear and anxiety in the unknown places of life. His grace carries me when I have lost the will, the drive, and the direction to keep moving forward.

Grace is the magnitude of God's love manifested in my life. It is His grace that covers me and shelters me from the fiery darts of the devil. His grace surrounds me with undeserved blessings. His grace is precious and plentiful. It never runs out. "Grace is the heart of God to do you good when you deserve it least."[25]

As I look about my world now, I realize I experience God's rich grace in many forms, but I can honestly say I have not always been sure of what God's grace is. Now something amazing and wonderful is happening to me. By God's grace, the Holy Spirit is opening my eyes and my heart to not just see His amazing grace but to experience His grace in a way I have never experienced it before. For sure, I pray I will never again have to walk the cold, dark, and terrifying road where I found myself in the fall and winter of 2012-2013. But I can honestly say I thank God for that experience. In an odd sort of way, it was an answer to my prayers. I know you must think

---

[24] "It is the Lord who goes before you. He will be with you; He will not leave you or forsake you. Do not fear or be dismayed." (Deuteronomy 31:8 ESV)

[25] http://www.desiringgod.org/books/five-points.

I am either lying or on the verge of needing to go back to Sheppard Pratt, but it is the truth. I am walking the same road the Apostle Paul trod. I understand more and more what he must have meant when he said, "Most gladly, therefore, will I rather glory in my infirmities, that the power of Christ may rest upon me (KJV). For the sake of Christ, then, I am content with weaknesses, insults, hardships, persecutions, and calamities. For when I am weak, then I am strong (ESV)"[26] Because of my suffering, I am freer now than I have ever been in my life! You would not be reading *Flying with One Wing* now if it had not been for the pain of suffering I endured. I will shout it from the mountaintops. God's grace is all I will ever need!

After searching myself and pondering over the issue of God's grace these past years, I must admit, I am still no closer to a definitive answer than I was when my quest first began. I know I have always been taught God's grace is His favor, but that word seems to lack so much and is so over-used. As I began writing this chapter, I thought I still could not put into one word what God's grace is, but then the Holy Spirit revealed that glorious word to me. God's grace is Jesus! Jesus is God's grace personified and magnified in the earth. Yes, His name is Jesus, and He supplies all I need to fly, even if I have to do it with one wing.

I could sing of His grace forever. Oh Lord, let me bask in the rays of Your grace. Let me be immersed in the ocean of Your grace. Let me soar on the wings of Your grace. Your grace is amazing. Your grace is sufficient to meet all my needs and fulfill all my desires.

Sufficient is a larger word for enough. In other words, when I have God's grace, I really do not need anything else. His grace is all I need to live my life to its fullest extent. Often, we feel we need other things and other people to complete our lives, but the truth of the matter is God completes us. We do not need to go anywhere else to find true love, peace, joy, or abundance. All of those things are found in God and in His grace. We do not need a perfect family, a perfect career, a perfect mind, or perfect health in order to live the perfect life, as long as we have a relationship with a perfect God. I have found that perfection is only found in my imperfection. As I submit my imperfections to Christ, He molds me and

---

[26] 2 Corinthians 12:9b

shapes me into the perfect image of Himself. Every day the Holy Spirit puts me on His loom and weaves perfectly the threads that are to form my life.

Finding out that my mind was not as perfect as I thought was quite devastating, and there are still times when the struggle between what is true and what is perceived as true, or what is true and what is a lie becomes a daily challenge. But I can honestly say, God's grace continues to lift me. His grace covers me and gives me joy. His grace propels me forward and keeps me through each day. Yes, God's grace truly is sufficient.

However, this idea of sufficient grace is not original to me. I learned it from the Apostle Paul. Many people remember Paul as a man of great faith who wrote most of the New Testament in the Bible and who served God's purposes with passion and tenacity. God used him mightily to advance the Kingdom of God. No doubt, Paul was also a man of great faith and prayer. I truly believe Paul and Jesus had a wonderful relationship. I believe Paul could ask and God would give it. He could seek and God would help him find it. And he could knock and God would open every door for him. Yes, from what I read, Paul and God were on pretty good terms. There is, however, one incident where it seemed Paul just could not get God to move on his behalf. It is found in 2 Corinthians chapter 12.

The word of God says the Apostle Paul was given a "thorn in his side." The Scripture does not say what the thorn was. But it seems obvious to me that it was somewhat of an annoyance, and it caused Paul much pain and suffering because he asked God three times to take it away. Three times! What do you do when you ask God for His help the first time and He does not respond? What about when you ask Him the second time and He seems not to be listening? Or three times and the answer is not what you were hoping to hear? Paul wanted the thing gone. He was tired of it, and I suppose he believed he did not need it. God, however, had a plan for the thorn. God's plan was not to take it away but to show Paul all he needed was the grace of God.

The word "grace" in 2 Corinthians 12:9 comes from the Greek word *charis,* and according to the *Strong's Concordance,*[27] it is the "merciful kindness by which God, exerting his holy influence upon souls, turns them to Christ, keeps, strengthens, increases them in Christian faith,

---

[27] Strong's G5485 - *charis*

knowledge, affection, and kindles them to the exercise of the Christian virtues." Pastor John MacArthur, in his teaching *The Sufficiency of God's Grace*,[28] describes grace as "a favor bestowed by God through His power to transform a person's life, starting with salvation and going from there."

As I look back to my traumatic episode of Friday, October 19, 2012, I can see the beginning workings of God's transformative grace. What I could not see, God saw. What I did not know, God knew. God looked deep into the wounds of my past, the pain of my present, and the broken places of my future and decided to fix me. He drew me closer to Christ so the pain would not overwhelm me as He chiseled away at the scar tissue that had formed from the wounds of my past and had gone unnoticed. God strengthened my faith to deal with those present-day painful places that had become my "normal" everyday experience. And then, God removed the scaly cataracts from my eyes so I could see what He was doing in me and where He was leading me. In other words, God was graciously performing spiritual surgery on me to make me brand new so I could live and not die. Recovery is indeed a process; but when God's grace is working in you and with you, you can be made whole.

---

[28] https://www.gty.org/resources/pdf/sermons/80-72.

Chapter Nine

FLYING WITH ONE WING

*"But they that wait upon the Lord shall renew their strength; they
shall mount up with wings as eagles" Isaiah 40:31a (KJV)*

Anxiety and depression are stubborn beasts that threaten to accompany
its victims for their entire lives. It has been over four years since my life
was drastically altered by suddenly falling headlong into the dark pit
of depression and anxiety. So much has changed. I suppose the most
important thing I have had to do is to take a deep, hard look at my life. I
have had to learn how to prioritize and strategize in order to realize peace
and joy. Finding the road to peace and joy is not always easy. Out of the
shadows, anxiety and depression can arise at any time. Just when I think
it is all over, the diabolical twins assault my mind and body and cause me
to feel as if no progress has been made at all. But the truth is, progress has
been made. Every battle fought, and every victory won in the world of
mental illness has brought me closer to the God I love and trust and has
allowed me to find out more about who I am. My battles, as well as my
victories, have helped to develop me in every area of my life. My journey
through depression and anxiety has been pain with a purpose.

Cora Jakes Coleman in her book *Faithing It*[29] talks about a tragic car
accident that proved to be a blessing in disguise. God blessed her to walk
away from the accident, but what she discovered while in the hospital
was something totally unrelated to the accident. God used that serious

---

[29] Cora Jakes Coleman. Faithing It: Bringing Purpose Back to Your Life. 23%. Loc
669 of 2843

car accident to reveal truth she was unaware of and to propel her to her purpose in life. It was the car accident that opened the door to her destiny. As a result, others are being blessed by her story. She has moved past the broken place and has stepped into her blessing. She says, "I could still be looking at the car accident, but I stepped into the purpose for the pain."[30]

It is amazing how God uses the painful and horrific things in our lives to bring about the best days of our lives. Only He can turn misery into majesty, pain into purpose, tragedy into triumph. My story is like Cora's. It wasn't a car accident that brought me to my purpose, but it was an accident, something I didn't plan nor was I looking to find. We do not know what life will bring us; it is full of uncertainty and unknown places. We have no knowledge of what lies beyond the present moment. All we can claim to know is that life is often challenging. We must learn to navigate through fear and failure, purpose and pain, adventure and wonder, and relationships and reality.

I think life can be compared to a theme park. Every attraction and every ride have been carefully designed for the purpose of enjoyment. Although rides are exciting and many people enjoy them, they can also be extremely dangerous. Therefore, each amusement ride is equipped with safety features—locks, belts, harnesses, stop buttons, etc. These features do not stop the ride from doing what it does but they ensure the safety of the joy-seekers while helping them to enjoy the ride. Like a theme park, life can whip you about, toss you around, and flip you over; but the irony is, in all of that, life is also meant to be enjoyed. Every day of life is a gift from God, and we should rejoice in it.[31] In God's grace, He has equipped our lives with safety features that will hold us, keep us, protect us from harm, and allow us to enjoy the life we have been given.

The first safety feature God provides is salvation through His Son Jesus. Jesus's sacrificial death on the cross protects us from the power that sin and death have over our lives. His death makes us acceptable to God and saves us from eternal damnation in hell. Without the safety that salvation provides, nothing else in life really matters. God's word says, "What good is it for someone to gain the whole world, yet forfeit their

---

[30] Ibid.

[31] "This is the day that the LORD has made; let us rejoice and be glad in it" Psalm 118:24 (KJV).

soul?"[32] The next safety feature that God provides is Scripture. We would not know Who God is or how to live our lives to the fullest if we did not have His word. Since God is the Creator and Maker of all things (visible and invisible), He is the only One Who knows how everything works and fits together. The Scripture is our manual for successful living. It opens our eyes to Who God is. It provides instruction on how to live life. It strengthens us for the journey and gives us hope for a brighter day. The final safety feature God provides are our supporters. It is true that God never leaves us, and it is also true that God surrounds us with family and friends. Loving and helpful supporters are necessary as we go through life. God created us for community, and no one can live life to the fullest without supporters. Supporters also extend beyond family and friends. I found myself needing these other supporters (who can sometimes show up in our lives as people we don't even know). They were prayer warriors, doctors, nurses, psychiatrists, therapists, psychologists, social workers, and administrators. These supporters, along with my family and friends, were used by God to help me make it through.

I am a recipient of His protecting grace. When life was hard, God cared for me. When my life took a turn and I found it upside down, God cared for me. He did not allow anxiety to destroy me because He cares for me.[33] By God's rich grace and mercy, He moved me past the accident scene and walked with me through the road of recovery. All I had to do was wait on Him.

---

[32] Mark 8:36
[33] "Cast all your anxiety on Him because He cares for you" 1 Peter 5:7 (NIV).

Chapter Ten

How to Fly with One Wing

"You have been knocked into a whirlwind. Your yesterday before October 19th was certain to you. Even if you were unhappy, you were sure of how to keep it moving. Now, your tomorrow is full of "what ifs". It is okay. Just choose to live in your today, and tomorrow will be all okay."[34]

Three months felt like several. Depression and anxiety had attacked me and upset my life as I knew it. I got to a point where I had to decide whether I would surrender to the illness and die or whether I would confront it on all fronts and keep living.

In the previous chapter, I mentioned safety features that God has graciously given us to keep us from harm as we go through the challenges of life. Now I want to show you how you can still fly, even if you have to do it with one wing. These are things I have learned. Some are spiritual in nature, while others are practical tips. I want to start with the spiritual instructions God has shown me—realize your insufficiency, rely on God's sufficiency, and rest in God's ability.

Spiritual Instructions

Realize Your Insufficiency

I can often be guilty of thinking I can do it all, but the truth of the matter is sometimes I need help. We are not super humans. We are weak

---

[34] Cianni's words to me on Friday, February 1, 2013.

in ourselves, and if we are to live our lives fully, we must realize our weaknesses. I had to accept my weaknesses and trust God with them. My strength and power were insufficient in this battle. The beasts of depression and anxiety were resistant to my human efforts. I could not wish them away. Positive thinking did not work. I had sunk so low and was so afraid that even trying to pray and/or read the Bible were futile. I had come to the end of my rope and did not know what to do, but it became both humbling and freeing to realize I was not in control. It was then that I was able to release the responsibility of being healed from my hands. When I came to this realization, I was in the perfect posture to understand the second principle in being able to fly with one wing.

Rely on God's Sufficiency

Being a woman in need of strength just to make it through each day, I cannot afford not to know the truse source of my strength. When I found myself in the dark pit of depression and anxiety, there was no way I could have handled it alone. I did not even know what it was in the beginning. How could I fix what I did not even know was broken? Realizing God is all-sufficient, even when I am not sure of what the problem is, was a big relief. I was in trouble and I needed strength beyond my own. I needed someone who could carry me through. I needed the all-powerful, all-knowing, all-sufficient God Who I had learned about in my childhood and Who I had been trusting for most of my life to step in and help me. There was no doubt that only God could get me out of this. I remember reading an article from Dr. David Jeremiah. He wrote, "Problems are situations engineered by God to bring us face-to-face with our deficiency so that we might view His sufficiency as the only alternative." I certainly agree with Dr. Jeremiah. I had come face-to-face with my little strength, my weak faith, and my dim hope. The view of myself was that of a small child in need of her parent. If I had not realized it before, I knew it then; God is sufficient. Everything I needed for this journey was found in Him, and I could trust His way and His will for my life. This was the road He carefully chose for me. I was on a purposeful road. It was difficult. It was challenging. It was dark and scary for me, but yet God's all-sufficient power took me through it day after day. If I was going to come out of this, it would be only because God had made the way.

As a result of my struggle, God became more real to me in so many ways. The Scriptures are ripe with metaphors of God, revealing His characteristics and faithfulness to His people through their struggles of life. One such metaphor of God found in the Bible is that of a shepherd. The Old and the New Testaments are filled with language revealing the shepherd-like qualities of God. As my Shepherd, the Lord had promised to lead me and guide me. He promised to feed me, to carry me and to protect me all the way. I did not have to fear any evil because the Lord was right by my side. The Lord gave me personal attention as if I was the only one in need of His help. Whenever I needed Him, He was right there. He knew me. He knew my pain. He knew my fears. He knew my sadness and where it had taken root. He knew everything about me, and day-by-day He sent His grace to heal me and make me whole. I have often been told to relax and release my problems to God, and that was exactly what I had to learn to do if I wanted to fly with one wing.

Rest in God's ability

As long as I would continue to strive back and forth between believing I could do this on my own and submitting myself to God's way of handling things, I would not have peace. It is one thing to recognize God is almighty and all-powerful over all things, but it is quite another thing to rest in that knowledge. I had to trust God completely. That meant trusting Him with going to Sheppard Pratt in the first place, following all the instructions from all the medical and mental health professionals, showing up every day, being willing to be vulnerable, and even taking the medications.

I had a decision to make. I could stay in this state of panic and fear and depression and wait to see how long it would last, or I could rest in God's ability to help me deal with whatever means were necessary to bring about my healing and deliverance. It would be God's ability not mine that would help me begin and transition through the process that would lead to wholeness. It was a process and continues to be, but God's ability to support and sustain me never ceases. His love, power, and strength are relentless. They never let me go. I am so very glad I surrendered my will to God's will. I am better today than I was years and years ago.

Practical application is necessary as we put our faith to work. Faith without works is dead. In addition to walking this walk spiritually, there were practical things I needed to learn how to do.

Practical Instructions

Recognize You Have a Problem

What is your body telling you? Listen to what it has to say. God's grace gives us warnings that are often ignored because we are just too busy to slow down and heed the warning. Unbeknownst to me, something was wrong with me, and I needed to be fixed. I had become unwilling to acknowledge when I was doing too much and when I needed to take a break. It was as if I thought I was made of steel. I worked a regular job, took care of a sick husband, took care of the business of my home, and tried to be there for others of my family. I engaged myself in three different ministries and barely took real vacations (the kind where you don't work at all). Slowly, but surely, my body and my mind were winding down. It was only a matter of time before they would just give up.

There were secrets buried deep in my mind. Things that I did not want to admit about me and about my life. October 19, 2012, was about me. It was about my healing. It was about finding my way. It was God giving me an opportunity to be free of all the things that had been holding me captive physically, mentally, emotionally, and spiritually. It was my time to rewind, release, and be refreshed.

Recognize You Need Help

It has been said, "Admitting you have a problem is the first step in fixing the problem."

Being able to fly with one wing meant I had to accept the fact I had a problem and needed help. Me, need help? The preacher, teacher, and faithful woman of God that others come to for help? Me, need help? Yes, I had a problem and I needed help. I am a helper, but even helpers need to be helped sometimes. My pride had gotten in the way of my asking for help. I had to learn that every battle is not mine to fight. Every person is not mine to help. I had to learn that "No" is an answer. I had to learn how to set boundaries and take time for myself. I had to learn the difference between selfishness and self-care. In many ways, I was taking care of others, but I was not taking care of me.

As an African American woman, I had been taught by others that I must be strong always. My spiritual upbringing taught me the same. However, I had become too strong to be weak. God's wisdom teaches me that it is not weak to need help. In fact, my greatest strength is found in being weak. That is when I let go and let God! His word points us in the direction of seeking His help and the help of others in order to be successful and prosperous in life. The truth was I could not do it all. I was not Wonder Woman, Superwoman, or even the Bionic Woman. I was God's woman, living in a human body, and I needed help.

Be Courageous

Get the help you need, even if you have to do it afraid. Courage is not the absence of fear; it is moving despite or against your fear.

Receive the Help

Going to Sheppard Pratt was a big decision and a big step for me. It meant meeting people I did not know and submitting myself to trusting them.

God will fulfill His purpose for us in His time.[35] We need only to trust Him.

---

[35] "The LORD will fulfill his purpose for me; your steadfast love, O LORD, endures forever. Do not forsake the work of your hands" (Psalm 138:8 NRSV).

EPILOGUE

THE DAY MY LIFE BEGAN ANEW

"Now He had to go through Samaria" John 4:4 (NIV)

It is odd how sometimes the worst day of your life can actually be the best day of your life and when what looks like the end can really be the great beginning. When the events of Friday, October 19, 2012, led to such fear, panic, darkness, and sadness, there was no way I could see the good in all that or even thank God for what had happened. Standing on the level of my brokenness, I could see nothing but pain and fear. The confusion and chaos that rose from that fall in the darkness of that early morning leg crap were symptoms of an inner darkness I had been unaware of. However, now that I am lifted high above that moment in time, I see God's blood-stained thread of grace intertwined between each tear I cried and every panic attack I endured. Those few days seemed like an eternity to me. I lived my life as if I was walking through a land mine, as if at any moment, something could explode; and I would be destroyed. But I was not destroyed, not at all. I walked through it, and I lived through it. It was my faithful God who held true to His promise to strengthen me, help me, and uphold me (Isaiah 41:10) that has led me to life anew.

That explosive moment on October 19th was not to kill me but to destroy all the hidden sin and brokenness of my life. It had to happen if I was to be made new. God would not build a new life on top of a broken foundation. He would first tear down all old perceptions, uproot hidden sin, and dig out past hurts in order to leave a new foundation on which to build a brand, new life for me. Bit-by-bit and piece-by-piece, God untangled the mess that had become my life and restore me to healthier, happier, and holier places. As painful and frightening as that episode was in 2012, I needed it to be part of my journey. It is what has helped build me. It is who I am. Without it, I would not be me. Yes, October 19th had to happen if I was to ever have brand new life. Unbeknownst to me, I had a divine appointment that would lead to a divine encounter with the Divine One. Since that day, the Holy Spirit has ordered my steps though the unfamiliar world of mental illness. And when He does, He leads me straight into God's glorious plan of healing and restoration, not just for my life, but for all of those who struggle with mental health issues. Care receivers and care givers alike of mental health-related issues can find hope and help in my journey. And the journey continues.

Printed in the United States
By Bookmasters